Foundations

of

Political Science 2021

R. L. COHEN

Humanities
ACADEMIC PUBLISHERS

ISBN: 978-1-988557-63-2 (Hardcover)
ISBN: 978-1-988557-64-9 (Ebook)

Published in New Zealand

A catalogue record for this book is available from the National Library of New Zealand.

Kei te pātengi raraunga o Te Puna Mātauranga o Aotearoa te whakarārangi o tēnei pukapuka.

Contents

CHAPTER 1

Key definition in Political Science

1.1 Governments and regimes

Political Science is defined as the social science that examines politics by means of the empirical method. **Politics**, from Greek *politiká* (affairs of the cities), is the activity through which people make, preserve and amend the general rules under which they live. Being a social science and concerning the management of our communities, politics is unavoidably connected to both conflict – a competition against opposing forces -- and cooperation – the act of achieving goals through collective action. That is, human beings are social animals, but they have different wants, needs, and opinions, so they differ in the decisions about the **rules** by which they live. These latter are thus essential for any social system, since rules help to determine who will win or lose future power struggles without having to resort to violence.[1]

---

[1] Roller, E. (2005), *The Performance of Democracies: Political Institutions and Public Policy*. Oxford University Press, Oxford.

Politics is a **process** and not an outcome: due to the inescapable presence of diversity and scarcity, not all conflicts in society can be resolved, so the process of setting rules can create disputes among the population. These disputes are at the basis of two essential concepts to understand politics: **authority** and **power**. The latter can be defined as the ability to influence others, so it may not necessarily be political, while the former is a form of **legitimate** power, which means that authority is itself the right to exercise power. That is, individuals acknowledge that society requires a form of common agreement to ensure that rules are upheld, so politics is connected to exercise of authority, such that Easton defines it as the "authoritative allocation of values."[2] Yet, to reach this agreement, it is essential that human beings cooperate one with another up to the point that political power can also be defined as "acting in concert" as done by Hannah Arendt[3].

The concept of legitimacy is essential to understand what **the State** – the current prevalent form of political organization of our societies -- is, since Max Weber defines it as a "human community that (successfully) claims the monopoly of the legitimate use of physical force within a given territory."[4] This means that other actors may use violence, but the state is the only actor legitimized to do so. To exercise its power, the State power must be organized, and in order to decide who is in charge of allocating citizens' different values, societies need a form of **government,** namely a system or an organization for exercising authority over a body of people.

Politics produce different kinds of governments according to the level of control and authority exercised by the government over its population. At one end of the spectrum, the government makes all decisions about how individuals live their lives, and citizens are powerless to

---

[2] Easton, D. (1976). "Theoretical approaches to political support.", Canadian Journal of Political Science, 9 (3), pp. 431-448.

[3] Phillips, J. (2013), "Between the Tyranny of Opinion and the Despotism of Rational Truth: Arendt on Facts and Acting in Concert.", New German Critique, 40 (2), 97-112.

[4] Weber M. (2004 [1919]), The Vocation Lectures. "Science as a Vocation". "Politics as a Vocation", Ed by David Owen D. and Strong T.B., Hackett Publishing Company, Cambridge.

push back. At the other end, there is an anarchic system where individuals make the decisions for themselves, and government does not exist. Hence, governments can exercise this authority in different ways, and the form of government, or the set of rules that regulate the operation of a government, are defined as the political **regime.** This latter defines only a form of government and must not be misunderstood with its negative connotation, namely regime as an authoritarian political system that restricts the people's liberties.[5]

The difference between 'government' and 'regime' is important. For example, the United States federal government is composed of the three main branches (**legislative, executive** and **judiciary**) and draws its powers from the Constitution, the President and federal courts. With the elections, citizens decide which party (**Democratic Party** or **Republican Party**) they want to direct these branches and who should be the President. Instead, regime defines the political institutional framework of the country. Examples of regimes can thus be "**democracy,**" "**authoritarian,**" or "**totalitarian.**" The United States system of governance, namely its regime, is a **democratic republic** style, and this does not change with the elections. Elections are made to select – and to replace – governments while they cannot change regime type. Hence, regardless whether Republicans or Democrats win the elections, the United States regime will remain a democratic republic.

Overall, we can find four main types of regime: democracy, theocracy, autocracy, and totalitarianism. A regime is **democratic** if it guarantees the people's basic liberties and rights. Democracy's etymology comes from the Greek word *demos* ("the people") and *kratos* (power), and this implies that any democratic system must be based on a **popular sovereignty**, namely the principle for which the authority of the state and its government are created and sustained by the consent of its people, who

---

[5] Dietrich, S. and Bernhard M. (2009). "State or regime? The impact of institutions on welfare outcomes." *The European Journal of Development Research*, 28 (2), 252-269.

are the source of political power.[6] This sovereignty can be exercised in two main forms.

First, in a democracy as self-government, citizens can be directly involved in politics and make the rules that govern themselves, as it was in the case in Athens, Greece. Today, direct democracy can be recreated in several ways, from deliberative assemblies, to direct decisional means such as referendum, or the initiative process. The method by which citizens can become directly involved on a single issue by voting directly on an issue and proposing new laws or amendments to a state constitution is referred to as a **referendum**.

Second, modern democracy does not necessarily require a direct involvement in politics by the whole populace. A democracy can also assume the form of a **republic**, namely a form of government in which the people hold the power, but they rule indirectly by means of their representatives. This form of representative **democracy**, supported by Madison in his *Federalist Papers*,[7] is adopted in the United States and defines a regime where politicians rule society according to the constitutional law on behalf of the citizenry, but where the people still retain power due to democratic procedures such as **elections**, **party system**, and the **division of powers**. However, this form of government is not necessarily democratic, since there could be republics where citizens do not hold sufficient institutional means to control the elites ruling the country.

On the contrary, a regime is defined as **authoritarian** if the government restricts some of the basic liberties enjoyed by the citizenry. In this regard, it is important to underline the difference between an authoritarian and a **totalitarian** regime. The former restricts only certain liberties of the population; it may also accept certain independent organizations and it does not necessarily rely on a strong ideology to influence the people's values. On the contrary, **totalitarianism** aims at controlling every aspect

---

[6] Held, D. (2006), *Models of Democracy*, Stanford University Press, California.
[7] Madison J. (1982 [1788]), *The Federalist Paper by Alexander Hamilton*, James Madison and John Jay, Bantam Books, New York.

of citizens' life and does not accept any independent organization.[8] As mentioned by Benito Mussolini, father of Italian **fascism**, in a totalitarian state there is "all within the state, none outside the state and none against the state."[9] While there are still several authoritarian regimes in the world, North Korea is the last totalitarian regime left.

Finally, a regime can also be a "**theocracy**," namely a political system where the government is controlled by religious officials who are regarded as divinely guided. Such government leaders are members of the clergy, and laws are not based on political constitutions but rather on religious law. This form of government was typical of early civilizations, and while the **Enlightenment** has rendered this regime obsolete in Western societies, some theocracies still exist in the Middle-East, such as in Saudi Arabia and Iran.[10]

1.2 Theories of power

While 'government' and 'regime' are terms that define the way political power is organized within a certain state, different theories exist concerning the way scholars believe power should be framed, of which we can find four main paradigms. First, there is the **pluralist theory**, for which, if elected, representatives manage to represent equally the different interests present in our societies. Their rule could be both democratic and respecting the people's liberty. **Pluralism** developed after the end of the Second World War and reached its height during the 1950s and 1960s, periods of economic and political development for the Western societies characterized by low social conflict.[11]

---

[8] Curtis, M. (1979), *Totalitarianism*, Transaction Publishers, New Jersey.
[9] Ibid.
[10] Cosgel M.M. & Miceli T.J, (2013), "Theocracy", *Working papers 2013-29*, University of Connecticut, Department of Economics.
[11] Dryzek J.S., Dunleavy P. (2009), *Theories of the Democratic State*, Palgrave Macmillan, Basingstoke.

During this time, scholars stressed the beneficial consequences of social diversity for politics, advocating for constitutional ways of accommodating this diversity on public policy issues. In this framework, group interest is the building block of politics, since this helps citizens develop their political skills and understand how democracy necessitates bargaining and compromise. For this framework to work properly, no group must be blocked from competing on equal terms with another one, and any category of people who share an interest must have the chance to form a group. Therefore, **pluralists** believed that electoral competition creates a ***polyarchy***, namely a government of minorities where elections are competitive. In this system, diverse groups have the opportunity to make themselves heard effectively in the political system with politicians relying on the electorate's support for their re-election.

Considering politics as the result of the mediation between the requests of competing groups, pluralists hold that representative procedures ensure the representation of a large number of influential groups, thus avoiding the concentration of power in the hands of few individuals, which was the theoretical pillar of the second paradigm, namely the **elitist scholars**. This literature developed with Italian sociologists such as Gaetano Mosca[12], Roberto Michels[13] and Vilfredo Pareto[14], but later developed also in the United States thanks to scholars such as Charles Wright Mills.[15] This philosopher maintained that the common man cannot control politics, since power is centralized in the hands of a political **elite** that makes the fundamental decisions for everyone. Therefore, Mills defined elites as: "those political, economic and military circles which,

[12] Renzo S. (1952). "Note on Gaetano Mosca.", *The American Political Science Review,* 46.2 (1952), 603-605.

[13] Michels R. (1915), *Political Parties: A Sociological Study of The Oligarchical Tendencies of Modern Democracy,* Hearst's International Library Company, New York.

[14] Pareto V. (1935), *A Treatise on General Sociology,* General Publishing Company, Memphis.

[15] Mills C.W. (1956), *The Power Elite,* Oxford University Press, Oxford.

arranged in a complex and stratified order, make decisions of at least national importance."[16]

Mills noticed that in the American society of his time, the greatest power existed in the economic, political, and military spheres.[17] These elites determined the direction of the state and reduced all minor institutions to below these top powers. Moreover, each sector extended and thickened its relations with the others, so there was a strong interdependence between them. The members of these elites could also be considered as a single whole, since they behaved in a benevolent way among themselves and had common interests with similar social origins. Therefore, despite the theory that democracies should spread political power equally, these elites ruled centralized power in their hands.

The power of the elites is connected to the third paradigm, namely the **bureaucratic theory**. This view relies on Weber's famous theory for which bureaucratization was intertwined with the development of the **territorial state** and the **capitalist economy**.[18] That is, the development of a mass citizenship increases both the quantitative demands on the state administration, and the qualitative demand for uniformity of treatment, which can only be met by a **supra-local** administrative system, operating on the basis of impartiality between persons. Hence, bureaucracy is a distinctive feature of the modern world because it constitutes an efficient structure of power and of administration over a large territory.

This process influences also the structure of democratic systems, since bureaucratization reduces the importance of the parliament in favour of the party, its leaders, and of specialized agencies. For example, the bureaucratic theory suggests that in the United States, those within agencies like the EPA, CIA, and the FBI, are the ones who have the real power within the nation. That is, '**democratization**' did not lead to a

---

[16] Ibid.

[17] Ibid.

[18] Lutzker, M. A. (1982), "Max Weber and the analysis of modern bureaucratic organization: Notes toward a theory of appraisal.", *The American Archivist*, 45 (2), 119-130.

great dispersal of power to the masses, even though this does not mean that parliament has become obsolete. Rather the opposite: certain democratic processes have become essential in politics, such as the selection of leaders by electoral competition, the provision through Parliament of a forum for public debate and review of policy, and a mechanism for removing leaders in the event of a serious loss of confidence.[19]

Finally, the last paradigm connected to political distribution of power is the **social movement theory**. This theory explains how social mobilization occurs, under which forms it manifests, and which political consequences it may have. This paradigm became particularly influential in the 1960s, when many in both the United States and Europe began to see civic protests as a means to improve politics. At first, these protests puzzled scholars because studies relied on a **deprivation theory** which taught that protests were a result of social sufferance, while social movements in the 1960s were the result of an increase in social welfare. Furthermore, answers to this puzzle created differences between American and European sociology.[20]

On the one side, American theories relied more on structural approaches that examined which social and political contexts enabled or restricted protests. Among the factors that increased political movements, scholars underlined features such as an increased access to political decision making power, an instability in the ruling elites, and a lower ability of the state to repress these actions. Moreover, resource mobilization was of particular importance, since the more organized a community, and the more material, moral, cultural and human resources it possessed, the more likely a protest was to begin.

On the other side, the European strand focused more on social-constructivist approaches that focused less on social-class and material

---

[19] Waters T, Waters D (2015), *Weber's Rationalism and Modern Society: New Translations on Politics, Bureaucracy, and Social Stratification*, Palgrave Macmillan, London.
[20] Morris, A. (2000), "Reflections on social movement theory: Criticisms and proposals.", *Contemporary Sociology* 29 (3), 445-454.

explanations, to argue instead that current protests are different from past labor movements based on social-class, since social movements are now based on post-material features as collective identity, gender, and sexuality. On top of that, recent scholars such as Goodwin and Polletta argued that emotions, construction of meaning and agency, play a significant part as well in leading to the formation of social movements.[21]

As described by these paradigms, power is not organized in the same way in each country and this has significant consequences, not only for the people's political power, but also for one of the pillars of any political system, namely the people's liberty.

1.3 Types of liberty

Overall, two main conceptions of liberty have dominated the political debate, namely Isaiah Berlin's division between a "**negative liberty**" and a "**positive** (or **organic) liberty.**"[22] Negative liberty, which is freedom from external restraint on one's actions, include such examples such as civil and political rights such as freedom of speech, life, private property, freedom from violent crime, freedom of religion, habeas corpus, a fair trial, and freedom from slavery. Positive liberty requires the agent to take an active part in gaining control of themselves, since it claims "I am free to the extent that I achieve self-mastery." Positive liberty mainly focuses on answering the question: "By whom am I ruled?" Therefore, the positive desire to govern myself is connected to the belief that it is essential to determine who is making the political decisions to assess if citizens are free or not. Hence, the main question on which this conception of liberty is framed is: "What does it mean to be free to govern myself?"

First, self-mastery entails that individuals must be a *subject* and not an *object*, namely a self-directed doer able to make decisions by herself

[21] Buechler, S. M. (1995). "New Social Movement Theories", *The Sociological Quarterly*, 36(3): 441-464.
[22] Berlin I. (1958), *Two Concepts of Liberty*, Oxford University Press, Oxford.

and not something moved by external forces. Being a subject is important because only insofar as I am able to conceive policies and goals of my own (and I am afterwards able to realize them), can I consider myself a self-mastered human being. Otherwise, I will just be an object, a mere 'thing' directed by others according to their needs. In this framework, I am free to the degree that I can realize my own will, while I am enslaved to the extent that I cannot do so.[23]

On the contrary, **negative liberty** is the concept describing individuals having a personal sphere that must not be constrained by any external interference – a space within which they can act unobstructed by others. Conceiving freedom in terms of non-interference, it becomes essential to understand which hindrances damage personal liberty and which could instead be accepted. The negative liberty scholars' answer to this dilemma has a pivotal social component, since they maintain that citizens are unfree if others prevent them from doing what they could otherwise do. Individuals are then politically unfree when – and only when – they are prevented from attaining a goal by another human being: the wider the area where they are not hindered by other human beings in exercising their choices, the freer they are[24].

At first glance, it may seem simple to guarantee this liberty in a framework where all coercion is conceived as bad because it represses human desires. Total freedom lacking coercion. However, the fact that we live in social systems, where personal liberties are inevitably connected, creates disputes among scholars regarding how many "bads" we ought to impose to avoid larger evils. The problem is then how wide each individual's personal sphere should be, since if everyone was given unlimited freedom, we would live in a chaos where the will of the stronger would prevail over that of the weaker. In a negative liberty framework, the argument is thus: the line between the area of private life and that of public authority

[23] Berlin I. (2002), *Liberty*, Oxford University Press, Oxford.
[24] Berlin 2002; 171-177.

should be drawn to have the maximum degree of non-interference compatible with the minimum demands of social life.

Thus, the negative liberty solution differs from the one given by positive liberty. Whereas the latter aims to put authority directly in the hands of the citizenry, the former focuses on finding a minimum area of personal freedom that cannot be violated by anyone, and by this means, they aim to block authority. Hence, these two views focus on two different aspects of power: whereas positive liberty scholars focus on the *source* of the power in the hands of those ruling the social system, negative liberty scholars address the problem of the *intensity and amount* of power that rulers ought to have.

Berlin's division has yet been criticized by the republican conception of liberty as non-domination, whose origins can be found in Rome and later in the commonwealthman tradition, with books such as *Cato's Letters* by Trenchard and Gordon[25] or Madison's essays in the *Federalist Papers*. This ideal centres around the threat of having to live at the mercy of another, since it maintains that liberty involves **emancipation** from any **subordination** under **domination**. That is, it is important to determine when a party 'A' is actually dominating party 'B.' According to Philipp Pettit, the answer is that 'A' is dominating 'B' if – and only if – the former practises interference at will and with impunity, thus posing an arbitrary imposition on the latter's life.[26]

Republican liberty as non-domination has two main features. First, liberty is the opposite of slavery, and even if the master were to be benign, 'living at the mercy of another' is considered a great evil to avoid. Second, if the interference is not arbitrary, but controlled by the interests and opinions of those affected, it is not a form of domination. This view cannot be represented by Berlin's dichotomy. On the one hand, the fact that I am free from the mastery of another individual has no direct connection with the achievement of my self-mastery. On the other hand,

[25] Trenchard J., Gordon T. (1971), *Cato's Letters*, Da Capo, New York.
[26] Pettit P. (1997), *Republicanism: A Theory of Freedom and Government*, Clarendon Press, Oxford.

republicanism focuses on a different X from which we should be free than the one chosen by negative liberty scholars, since the latter think that X should be "interference," whereas the former maintain that it ought to be "mastery."[27]

For this reason, there are two main differences between non-domination and non-interference. First, if one individual is subjected to a master, even though she does whatever she likes, thus enjoying non-interference, she is still a slave, since it is the opportunity to interfere at will that gives the dominating power to the master, despite whether or not the master will eventually use it. The problem of non-interference is even though the master may let the slave decide freely under some conditions, the slave will never be free. Conversely, non-domination grants greater security to personal freedom, since the master cannot interfere with the individual in any case.[28]

Second, interference may occur without people being rendered thereby unfree, since no domination exists if one interferes with my liberty but does so according to my will. Conversely, non-interference entails that every interference limits people's set of choices of some degree, and as such it constrains their freedom. Some interferences in people's lives are thus acceptable, especially if a third party interferes in a relationship where A dominates B to defend and free the latter. This aspect is central in relation to the rule of law, since it entails that a proper law is a non-mastering interferer if it does not compromise the people's liberty. On the contrary, in a non-interference framework, the fact that each law is an interference creates a difficult puzzle for the state, since its actions are seen as an inevitable constraint on an individual's set of choices.

[27] Pettit 1997; 52-61.
[28] Pettit P. (2012), *On the People's Terms: A Republican Theory and Model of Democracy*, Cambridge University Press, Cambridge.

CHAPTER 2

American Political Culture

2.1 American Political Culture

American political culture is unique and different from all other countries in the world. American political culture is built upon values that limit the power of government. **Political culture** is a set of *shared* ideas, values, and beliefs that define the role and limitations of government and people's relationship to that government. The American political culture is woven together from political narratives that are vastly different across the nation. Every state has unique stories and a history defining the political narrative. We also see many instances when states do not get along or cooperate, and in these instances, cultures clash. Take, for example, the American Civil War, arguably the darkest and bloodiest hour in the country's history. That conflict represented an enormous fracturing in the political culture. The Union states maintained one set of beliefs on slavery, tariffs, suffrage, and government power, whereas the Confederates held diametrically opposite views. For years, the United States was divided on the most fundamental aspects of political culture, and it culminated in war. It was a loss of social cohesion that led to widespread suffering. This is one of the most critical reasons for studying the topic of American political culture and developing a better understanding of its dynamic input and output functions.

It is impossible to provide a tangible understanding of the American political culture. The political culture is unembodied and unspoken. Disparate views abound, especially with things based on personal experiences and exposure to other cultures. Those who have not traveled or met many people from other countries are more likely to think that the beliefs they share are objective reality, not just one set of many optional sets of narratives. In the political science subfield of comparative politics, scholars research other countries and discover widely different values on everything from group identification, to suspicion of government, to tolerance of outside cultures. Examining these differences is one the primary methods researchers use to analyze societies objectively, avoid ethnocentrism, and disseminate information for learning purposes.

Political culture is easiest to recognize when one steps outside of it. Being inside of a political ideology or system can keep a person from seeing the 'big picture' of the political system. Political culture gives people a common set of assumptions about the world and a common political language within which they can agree.

2.2 Fundamentals of American political culture

American political culture is defined by the concept of limited government. **Limited government** is the political philosophy of a government limited in power. This is a key concept in the history of liberalism. **Liberalism** is a school of thought derived from the Enlightenment, found particularly in thinkers such as John Locke. Locke's beliefs in limited government were the inspiration for the **Declaration of Independence** and the primacy of "life, liberty, and the pursuit of happiness." One might notice the similar sounding of the words "liberty" (from the Latin "*libertas*", meaning freedom from despotic control) and "liberal" (meaning free from restraint in speech or action). Each of these terms, in their most classical sense, refer to freedom and an aversion to external coercion. Locke and his adherents, like Thomas Jefferson, wrote in a time when many began to bring into question the legitimacy of the old, sometimes despotic, European monarchies.

American political culture focuses on **individualism** more than **collectivism**. Individualism has an emphasis on individual rights rather than on the collective whole. Individualism is the idea that individuals, not society, the community, or the government, are responsible for one's own well-being.

In American society, we hold the expectation that people will provide for their own forms of retirement and social welfare. Other countries, such as Great Britain, embrace community and communitarianism, insisting that people be protected by the government. For those people who prefer to have a social democracy, or community-focused democracy, the public interest is best served when all of society uses the government as a mechanism to take care of its citizens through things such as universal healthcare and a social welfare system. In the United States, with individualism, it is not the government's responsibility to provide for full coverage of one's retirement, well being, or employment.

American political culture provides a belief in core values of freedom, equality, and representative democracy, in a context of minimal government coercion so that the political culture ensures that the people have true 'freedom.' **Freedom** is understood by Americans as freedom *from* government. **Equality** in America is equality under the law. All forms of equality that require minimal governmental intervention. What is the origin for the concern for equality in modern political culture? In 19th century France, the motto of "liberte, egalite, and fraternite" (liberty, equality, and fraternity) became a chief concern after the violent French Revolution. Philosophers like Jean-Jacques Rousseau and Maximilien Robespierre emphasized equality as an important ingredient in forming a social contract between members of society. Equality paves the way for the possibility of thriving democratic republics.

Equality, defined, expresses that all citizens enjoy the same privileges, statuses, and rights in the eyes of the law. Social equality means that all individuals enjoy the same lawful status in society. Social equality is where the political/social hierarchy is free from institutional nobility. This would bar the existence of titled privileges such as those of barons or archdukes who inherit special benefits when they are born. Civil servants in the government are elected or appointed based on the law rather than heredity. Political equality is the means that every citizen has the same political rights and opportunities. This includes **suffrage** (voting) but it also includes the right to **due process** (trial by jury, right to an attorney). Although America has a dark history of universal suffrage being denied to anyone other than white landowning property owners, the United States has made great strides to create political and social equality for all people. Equality also is considered to be economic equality. Economic equality focuses on the differences in wealth. Social critics scrutinize wealth/income inequality out of concerns for justice and the loss of quality of life for those with less wealth. Others counter this by claiming that some inequality is unavoidable and that equality under the law is the only thing worth safeguarding. At any rate, the issue of equality, social, political or economic, retains an important point of divergence in today's political culture.

2.3 Democracy in American Political Culture

Democracy is a decision-making process by which individuals register their preferences for their rulers (and the policies they promise). A democracy is a government which citizens rule directly and make government decisions themselves. In a democracy, the citizens have power over their government's decision making.

Is the United States considered a democracy? Yes, in some sense, but it is important to maintain precision of terms. With some exceptions (see the next section), the United States is not what you would call a "direct democracy," but rather a constitutional republic or representative democracy. Aristotle was one of the first to use the term "republic," which accounts for the United States and most countries in western civilization today. Under this model, citizens participate in politics by voting on representatives (members of Congress, the Senate, the President) who are expected to carry out the general will of those they govern. Elected officials, even your local mayor or councilmember, have a fiduciary responsibility to govern with the best interests of the people in mind. They are held accountable electorally. If they fail to satisfy their constituents, or are found guilty of a scandal, they run the risk of getting voted out of office.

In a democracy, the use of referendum can allow citizens to have direct access to creating a democratic state. A referendum is an election in which citizens vote directly on an issue. This is a way to employ "direct democracy." California passes laws and removes people from office with this method. An example of this, in 2020, was Proposition 17. This gave citizens the opportunity to vote on a referendum regarding voting rights for convicted felons released on parole. In that instance, it passed with 58% of Californians voting in favor.

In a democracy, we would assume a social, political, and economic equality amongst the people. Equal opportunity is the idea that every American has the same chance to influence politics and achieve economic success regardless of their race, gender, or class. It is the American dream that anyone can pull themselves up by their bootstraps, rich or poor, and have the same opportunities as anyone else. In the American political culture, the attitudes, beliefs, and assumptions that we create give order and meaning to public life. In a democracy, the American political culture gives Americans the ability to disagree but remain united ultimately.

2.4 American Political Ideologies

America has several different political ideologies. In modern times, it may feel like the competing political ideologies are polarized and in constant disagreement. **Ideologies** are the competing narratives we create to explain those disagreements. Typically, ideological division in the United States has been along economic terms, disputes between conservatives and liberals. Sometimes the disputes involve social dimensions as well though.

In the American political spectrum, **conservatives** on the right call for less regulation of the economy (lower taxes, freer trade, unrestricted competition). Conservatives are Americans who believe in reduced government spending, personal responsibility, traditional moral values, and a strong national defense. It is common to see conservatives known as "right wingers." Liberals are the second political group in the American political spectrum. **Liberals** on the left call for more government regulation (like social welfare programs, universal health care, and free preschool programs). Liberals value cultural diversity, government programs for the needy, public intervention in the economy, and individual's right to a lifestyle based on their own social and moral positions. Modern liberals may differ from the Locke's classical emphasis on abundant liberty, but they still emphasize social liberty, couched within a need to safeguard society with economic safety nets. For example, a modern liberal would be socially-libertarian on something like drug possession, preferring not to criminalize it, but would seek state intervention on economic measures such as Social Security, a regulatory safety net.

Starting in the 1960s and 1970s, however, other non-economic issues started to motivate voters—issues like racial desegregation, civil rights, women's rights, including reproductive rights, prayer in school, and reducing crime. These issues split Americans along a political dimension much like a vertical line. When you combine the horizontal, economic ideological dimension with the vertical, social ideological dimension, you get four ideological categories that are important for understanding American politics today.

2.5 A closer look at American ideologies

American ideologies are distinct along economic lines. American **economic conservatives** are those that believe in the narrative that the government that governs best, governs least. Proponents of this ideology want to see the government provide less oversight on fiscal policy. An example of a political ideology that believes in less oversight is libertarianism.

Libertarians believe in minimal government. They tend to favor policies like gun rights, reproductive rights, civil rights, assisted suicide, and legalized marijuana. Most want only as much regulation of the economy as it would take to keep competition fair and the market from tanking. Robert Nozick, author of *Anarchy, State, and Utopia*, gives the model of a "night-watchman" state, where the government exists only for the most basic functions. It would go no further than minimal governance such as police, courts of law, and a small military. This model omits most state intervention into economic and social matters.

The economic liberal, on the other hand, seeks to utilize the government to empower people who may be disadvantaged. **Economic liberals** are distinguished from economic conservatives by two beliefs. They see citizens not just as individuals but as members of groups, some of whom are often not treated equitably by society. The second ideology is they believe government action may be necessary for all people to reach their full potential. Economic liberals favor economic policies that would provide a basic standard of living to all individuals.

The progressives are those who are on the most extreme left end of political ideology. **Progressives** are those who are the farthest to the left on the political continuum. Economic liberals are those who believe in an even stronger role for the state in creating equality. Progressives made a substantial impact in America around the turn of the 20th century under the leadership of presidents like Theodore Roosevelt and Woodrow Wilson. This was during a time when the United States saw an expansion in population, industrialization, and urbanization. Progressive critics, like Upton Sinclair, believed that this coincided with an increase in corruption, business monopoly, and worker exploitation. The response to this was the creation of several new government bureaucracies such as the Food & Drug Administration (FDA), the United States Department of Agriculture (USDA), the Federal Trade Commission (FTC), and the passage of the 16th Amendment, which enabled the income tax. This would eventually go on to include the Prohibition of alcohol with the 18th Amendment. The biggest takeaway from this era was the bipartisan

(Republicans and Democrats) embracing of a more hands-on and active approach to governance.

Social issues are a source of division between conservatives and liberals as well. **Social conservatives** put a priority on the government preserving a traditional social order. Social conservatives include several groups who believe that their vision of the social order (that is, how people should live their lives) is absolute and want to put it into law. Social conservatives receive some of the intellectual foundation for their views in the works of the Irish philosopher/statesman, Edmund Burke. Burke, as opposed to Rousseau, was more suspicious of the concept of social contract because he thought it would lead to the disintegration of tradition and customs. Social conservatives seek to enact protective laws for maintaining social norms but are wary of what they consider to be the "social engineering" of social liberals.

Social liberals have concrete ideas about what they think is right and don't mind stepping on civil liberties if necessary to realize them. The social liberal doesn't always gain many adherents because it pushes the limits of Americans' limited government, individualistic culture. There are some occasions, however, when social liberals can make an impact. Whenever a perceived crisis gains public visibility (i.e., the Vietnam War or the Civil Rights Era), social liberals may have a chance to persuade the public to vote to enact legislative changes that contradict the prevailing social milieu. Exceptional circumstances notwithstanding, since we tend towards limited government, Americans distrust the government and place limits on the authority the government can exercise over people.

As you can see, political culture is manifest in many shapes and forms. You have probably encountered friends, family, and opponents who represent some or all of these viewpoints. It is not difficult to see how the competing sub-cultures might clash as they did during the American Revolution, the American Civil War, the Civil Rights Era, and perhaps today as federal, state, and local elections continue to be contentious. With this framework for comprehending political culture, we can learn about the current political context. What are the major points of contention between social conservatives and social liberals? How do they fuel the debate over the hot-button political issues (war, abortion, drug restrictions, education costs, etc.)? Can we reconcile these cultural differences without incurring violence and civil wars? How do individualists and communitarians get along under the umbrella of the same government? Understanding political culture is a useful way to make sense of the various political forces at play in American civic life.

C H A P T E R   3

Politics and Economic Models

3.1 Politics and economics

Why would the discussion of economic models and politics occur intertwined?

The first answer to why these two fields are connected is that human beings are a social species. That is, each individual defines her own needs and desires in cooperation with others, so we must find a way to socially organize these relations. If we lived in a world where resources are infinite, this would not be necessary, since all citizens could just fulfil any of their desires as they please. However, in our empirical world **scarcity** plays an essential role. This refers to the fact that human and non-human resources are finite and society is thus only capable of producing a limited amount of goods.[29] In short, there are not sufficient resources to produce all the wares that people desire or want to consume. For this reason, societies have to find a way to redistribute the limited amount of goods and wares at their disposal. This is the role of **economics**, which is defined as the process for deciding who gets the material resources and how they get them. Hence, economic goods are those wares that are relatively scarce and need to be allocated according to a certain criterion.

---

[29] Hahnel R. (2003), *ABCs of Political Economy. Modern Primer*, Pluto Press, London.

Economics is a social science not only because it concerns the way society organizes itself to provide good to its citizens, but also because it aims to explain the economic behavior - how these latter exchange scarce resources - of individuals, groups and organizations. To do so, economics relies on the **rational choice theory**, namely the conception for which economic agents take their decisions according to what they mostly prefer and to the hindrances they encounter and the aggregate behavior in society reflects the sum of the choices made by individuals. At the individual level, this means that the agent evaluates the alternative options she encounters in terms of costs and benefits, choosing the one whose outcome offers the most amount of benefits and the least amount of costs[30].

At the aggregate and social level, economics assumes that each economic agent knows the economic model and that her actions are consistent with what decision-makers would do in a situation with the same nature, amount of information and social structure. This is the **rational-expectations theory**, which is not only an assumption related to present behavior of economic agents, but also an assumption regarding their future decisions and the fact that even if agents may not be perfectly correct, they will be right on average over time. In this regard, rational-expectations theory is slightly different from the rational choice theory. Whereas the latter concerns how individuals take decisions, the former is an assumption about the economic system, since it maintains that over time and on average, economic agents tend to be correct.[31]

Overall then, economics concerns the decision related to how to allocate the resources. To do so, we must create some forms of social institutions, namely a social arrangement by means of which we decide how to satisfy our needs and desires. This is where politics intervene and become intertwined with the economy: politicians influence the types

---

[30] Sen, A.K. (1982), *Choice, Welfare and Measurement,* Blackwell, Cambridge.
[31] Gourieroux, C., Jacqueline Pradel J. (1986), "Direct test of the rational expectation hypothesis", *European Economic Review,* 30 (2), 265-284.

of economic decisions implemented by deciding how assets are utilized in our economy. The goal for politics is then to decide which economic system better fulfils the economic needs of our communities.

Throughout history, societies have created different social institutions to organize citizens' needs and desires by assigning in different ways duties and economic rewards to individuals according to how they participate in the economy. Of all the different typologies, two economic systems in particular have framed the way economics is shaped nowadays, capitalism and socialism.

Capitalism

Capitalism is usually defined as an economic regime where enterprises and/or private citizens own the means of production and where employers pay a wage to their employees to manufacture goods with the purpose of afterwards selling them to produce profits. Even though these general traits are usually largely accepted in the literature, there is not a specific definition of capitalism that is unanimously accepted, so it is difficult to trace back its origins. If one argues that capitalism is simply the most natural way to allocate resources within an economic community, then it has always existed and it is an intrinsic feature of human beings. That is, human beings' nature is made of the will to enrich oneself or her community, so capitalism has always existed and will always exist. Yet, others argue that capitalism is not related to human beings' nature, but it rather developed as a result of specific economic phenomenon, such as the development of agriculture, or slavery in ancient societies. Hence, capitalism is a precise historical feature that has not always existed and it will not necessarily last forever[32].

That said, there is a widespread agreement concerning the fact that capitalism is an economic system where production is not planned by a

---

[32] Weingast B., Wittman D.A. (2006), *The Oxford Handbook of Political Science*, Oxford University Press, New York.

central government, but it is dictated by laws of **demand and supply** – defined as the economic relationship between the amount of a commodity that producers want to sell at a certain prince and the quantity consumers wish to buy - in the market economy. The term **market** is thus central to capitalism and it refers to decision making of multiple individuals about what to buy or sell, which creates different levels of demand and supply.

This is also how price is determined, since **prices** represent the equilibrium point at which the quantity of goods supplied by producers equals the amount required by consumers. More in detail, prices represent the compensation – usually measured in a certain currency - given by consumers to producers in return for one unit of goods or services. Prices are thus influenced by different factors that do not remain constant over time, such as production costs, demand of the product and availability. These features rather change continuously causing another important economic process, namely **inflation**, which is the decline of purchasing power of a given currency over time. Inflation is not a completely random process, but it is possible to quantify according to changes in the increase of an average price level and a basket of selected goods and services over time. The opposite may occur as well, since a deflation period results in an increase of the purchasing power of money over time.

Inflation does not only affect consumers' purchasing power, but it also changes financial mechanisms such **currency exchange rates**, holding costs and bank loans. For what concerns exchange rates, namely the amount of currency needed in a specific country to buy the same unit of another country's currency (how many $ you need to buy 1 euro), money supply and interest rates strongly influence the demand for a currency. This is an important aspect of the economy, so governments and their central banks use interest rates as a tool to control their domestic currency and thus their economy.

For what concerns the banking system, banks both pay an **interest rate** on the people's savings in order to attract depositors and they receive an interest rate for the money that is loaned from their deposits. When interest rates are low, businesses and individuals are more inclined to ask for loans. Banks respond to these requests by offering more loans, which increases the money supply in a fractional reserve banking system. This results in a growing money supply that increases inflation, which means that more money will be needed to buy the same unit of goods and services. These processes may be unstable if left on their own, so governments create specific economic institutions – such as the Federal Open Market Committee – to regulate interest rates as a means to keep inflation rates under control and to maintain a balanced economy.

This is an oversimplified explanation of why interest rates and inflation tend to be inversely correlated, but it well describes why even in capitalist systems there may be the need for governmental and/or private interventions. For example, one of the economic tasks implemented by governments is to use taxes to balance economic inequalities, to fund public services and also to encourage or discourage certain behaviors. That is, taxes can be seen to serve a similar function to that of prices in private transactions, namely they can determine what actions should be done by governments and who will pay for them. There are different ways to do so and one of these is the **benefit principle,** for which resources should be allocated by the public sector directly according to consumer wishes. Conversely from private transactions, this principle is difficult to implement because citizens do not want to pay for a public service if they can be excluded from its benefits, so many important aspects of welfare could be negatively affected in this way.[33]

From this brief description, it follows that capitalism is not a monolith, but it presents itself in many facets and forms in political science. As aforementioned, all scholars agree that capitalism is the economic regime where capital goods belong to private citizens, but since the way it is organized has differed significantly over time, there have been different visions related to what capitalism actually is. Due to this difficulty in

---

[33] Frank, R.H. (2000), "Why is cost-benefit analysis so controversial?", *The Journal of Legal Studies*, 29 (2). 913-930.

defining what capitalism precisely is, there has never been an academic agreement on its 'political economy', but rather many different perspectives on some specific questions related to its ethics, equality and morality. More pertinent to the economy, there has always been a debate on how much we ought to regulate markets.

On the one hand, there are those sustaining a **Laissez-faire capitalism**, for whom capitalist markets should be completely free from any economic interventionism such as subsidies and regulations. This view is based on two pillars. First, on an integral conception of freedom as non-interference for which individual economic liberty must not be curtailed by the state's intervention. Second, that markets are capable of self-regulating and that best results are thus achieved when the market is left to its spontaneous order.[34] Hence, there is no space for government intervention in the economic sector. Laissez-faire developed in the 18th century, but this view is still influential, since **neoliberalism** - one of current the dominant economic paradigms - has drawn from it most of its structural features.[35]

On the other hand, most scholars acknowledge that we should have forms of **regulated capitalism** to control markets in a certain way, even though decision-makers should mainly be individuals rather than public agents as the government. In this system, individuals may decide they want the government to step in to regulate behaviors that are not in the public interest and to fix externalities created by economic liberty. As for previous features, the spectrum of "how much" government ought to intervene is wide and can be differently connected to capitalism. Yet, another important economic theory, socialism, maintains that it is not a matter of regulating capitalism, since we can reduce capitalism's problems only insofar as governments keep total control of the economy.

---

[34] Hill, L. E. (1964), "On Laissez-Faire Capitalism and Liberalism'.", *The American Journal of Economics and Sociology*, 23 (4), 393-396.
[35] Ganti, T. (2014), "Neoliberalism.", *Annual Review of Anthropology*, 43, 89-104.

Socialism

Socialism is defined as an economic system where there is a social owner-ship of economic means of production, together with a planned market economy. According to Marx, forms of planned and public economy can be traced back up to primitive human-gatherer societies, but it is only with the modern era that this theory proposed itself as the alternative response to capitalism.[36] This latter commodifies land, means of produc-tion and work to create profit, but this can be seen as opposite to the fabric of society. Some scholars thus started pointing out that the prob-lem of capitalism was private property, since they maintained that even if we control and 'tame' private property with the rule of law, the fact that some individuals own the means of production unavoidably leads to the exploitation of those who do not own them.[37]

Capitalism was thus seen as contrary to human needs such as cre-ative work, diversity, solidarity and satisfaction of needs. As a response, socialism aimed at structuring an economic system more compatible with these economic needs. At first, socialism was more a utopian ideal. Analyzing workers' poor conditions, some scholars – such as Shaker's Christian socialism or the Hutteriti in the United States - maintained that the source of workers' problems was that they were working in large factories exploited by their employers. On the contrary, the solution was to be found in small communities that would have resolved material scarcity by structuring societies on a commune spirit. Hence, this first period lacked a proper economic theory and was mainly based on uto-pian ideas.[38]

The first glimpses of an economic theory that promoted equal-ity as a way to achieve a meritocratic society arose with the anarchist

---

[36] Saitta, D. J. "Marxism, prehistory, and primitive communism.", *Rethinking Marxism*, 1 (4), 145-168.

[37] Brenkert, G. G. (1979), "Freedom and private property in Marx.", *Philosophy & Public Affairs*, 122-147.

[38] Bestor A. (2018), *Backwoods Utopias: The Sectarian Origins and the Owenite Phase of Communi-tarian Socialism in America, 1663-1829*, University of Pennsylvania Press, Pennsylvania.

Pierre-Jospeh Proudhon, or with anti-capitalist scholars such as Robert Owen and Charles Fourier.[39] Yet, it was Henri de Saint-Simon who first coined the term "socialism" as the alternative system to capitalism who could have granted equal opportunities to the people.[40] Finally, socialism became a proper economic theory thanks to the famous work of Karl Marx and Friedrich Engels "Das Kapital" (Capital),[41] where it is possible to find the basis of the main socialist economic concepts, such as:

- *Marxist theory of value*: capitalism produces a multitude of goods, the value of which is mainly determined by the amount of work required to manufacture it;

- *Historical ownership relationship:* capitalism changed the owner-ship of the means of production, since whereas peasants used to own the tools of their job, urban workers were employees who have to sell the only thing they own, namely their work;

- *Commodity fetishism and economic exploitation:* workers are the source of economic value and the bourgeoisie, who own the means of production, exploits this value by transforming into profit the plus value coming from workers.

- *Capital accumulation:* capitalism is inherently led to continuously accumulate wealth by gaining from investments' returns and by profiting from workers' plus value. For this reason, capitalism must continuously find new markets and opportunities to expand itself world-wide and to repeat the accumulation process.

- *Crisis and centralization:* capital accumulation cyclically finds social and economic barriers that lead to periods of crisis which

---

[39] Prichard, A. (2013), *Justice, order and anarchy: The international political theory of Pierre-Joseph Proudhon,* Routledge, London.

[40] Simon, W. M. (1956), "History for utopia: Saint-Simon and the idea of progress.", *Journal of the History of Ideas* 17 (3), 311-331.

[41] Marx K. (2019 [1867]), *Das Kapital (Capital) A Critique of Political Economy*, Benediction Classics, Oxford.

often result in further centralization of the means of production in the hands of fewer capitalist;

In this framework, class conflict is an inherent characteristic of the economic system that according to Marx could be fixed only with a revolutionary movement aimed at the abolishment of private property so as to favor public property as the means of production. After Marx, other scholars not necessarily connected to socialism – such as J.S.Mill and J.M.Keynes – acknowledged that capitalism was unstable and that if the economic system was to 'tame' social conflict and to produce better results both in the different economic fields and in the market, it required some form of public intervention.[42] This debate on the connection between public intervention and market liberty has been a central feature of political economic debate over the last century, even though there currently are almost no countries framed on an integral socialist model.

Nowadays, we identify a **socialist economy** as a system where commodities are produced directly to be used, rather than to be sold to create profit. A central feature of the socialist economy is that it is **'planned'** which means that economic inputs are assigned directly by using resources to produce value according to the needs. This is opposite to what happens in a market economy where value is assigned indirectly by letting the market and economic cycles decide the inputs. A planned economy requires the public ownership of the means of production, even though this varies from a complete ownership by the state (statalism) to mixed forms of ownership by workers' cooperatives and a common property by all society.

Socialist industries do not encompass hierarchical relationships, but should be based on workers' self-government where each worker has the same decisional power over collective decisions as others.' Yet, most

---

[42] Taylor Q. (2016), "John Stuart Mill, Political Economist: A Reassessment", *The Independent Review*, 21 (1), 73-94.

historical examples of socialist countries, such as the Soviet Union or Yugoslavia, framed the management of their factories on a rigid bureaucracy that implemented the will of the state, thus leading to the debate related to whether or not such states were actually economically socialist or "collectivist bureaucrats."[43]

Aim of socialism is thus to 'neutralize' the capital by tying investments and capital to a social planning aimed at eliminating the economic cycle and the overproduction crisis typical of economies that rely on private property. In this way, socialist theorists maintain that workers could obtain more equality, freedom to access the resources they need to live and they would not be exploited of the value produced by their work. Over the last century, there have been several attempts to implement socialist economy in practice, even though most of them encompass certain capitalist features such as salaries given to employees and forms of partial free market.

Most of the social historical examples were structured on an economy planned by a central government who decided the kind and amount of commodities that had to be produced, as it was the case in the Soviet Union, in the Vietnamese socialist republic or in Cuba. This economic regime reached its peak in the 80s, when almost 1/3 of the total world population lived underneath such economic regimes, even though all these economies together generated only 15% of world's GDP. However, with the dissolution of the Soviet Union in 1991, countries steadily changed their economies to more liberal forms, such that nowadays only a few countries – Cuba, North Korea, China – adopt this economic regime and aside from North Korea, this socialism is more liberal than the central planned version of the Soviet Union.[44]

---

[43] Verdery, K. (1996), *What was socialism, and what comes next?*. Princeton University Press, Princeton.

[44] Sabry, M. I. (2017), *The Development of Socialism, Social Democracy and Communism: Historical, Political and Socioeconomic Perspectives*, Emerald Group Publishing, Bingley.

3.2 Political-Economic Systems

Since the dissolution of the Soviet Union, the vast majority of the countries in the world has adopted various forms of capitalism and this has created different debates. The first aspect that has often been debated in political economy is the connection between capitalism and democratic systems. A **capitalist democracy** is a country that has both a democratic government – a rule of law, democratic elections and that guarantees political liberty - and a capitalist economy with an emphasis on free markets and private enterprises.[45]

These political systems usually have a welfare system to make sure that citizens' basic rights are guaranteed, but at the same time they emphasize economic liberty and they rely on free-markets to create the innovation and competitiveness required for a prosperous social and economic development. Overall then, several scholars in social sciences – such as Przeworski, Lipset, Huber, Sen and many others – have studied the connection between democracy and economic development, finding that while it is not possible to maintain that economic development causes democratization, there is a positive correlation between democracies and economic development.[46]

Most western societies have adopted mixed forms of democratic capitalism. On the contrary, other regimes have implemented more stringent economic policies. This is the case of **authoritarian states** where there is no political plurality and where governments dispose of a strong central power that they use to reduce the rule of law, the separation of powers and many other democratic liberties. Even though there are different forms of these regimes - some may be dominated by a military, while others may be based on a religious theocracy or on the control of a

---

[45] Weingast & Wittman 2006; 603-618.
[46] Baum, M. A., Lake D.A. (2003), "The Political Economy of Growth: Democracy and Human Capital", *American Journal of Political Science*, 47 (2), 333-347.

strong political party - all these typologies have in common the fact that they hold a strict control over the economic system.[47]

This control over society is even more stringent in **totalitarian states** – such as the Nazi regime and the Soviet Union - where every aspect of the people's lives is under control of a central power. Therefore, while an authoritarian state hinders democratic liberties but it may guarantee certain freedoms to its citizens, there is no independent organization in a totalitarian state. For example, whereas there are still many authoritarian countries around the world, North Korea is the only actual totalitarian regime left.

---

[47] Somndrol P.C. (1991), "Totalitarian and Authoritarian Dictators: A Comparison of Fidel Castro and Alfredo Stroessner", *Journal of Latin American Studies*, 23 (3), 599-620.

CHAPTER 4

Federalism

What is federalism? Federalism is the division of governmental power among the various public jurisdictions. In antiquity, government was much more unitary or "top-down" in its execution and delivery. Before power-sharing arrangements became common, political systems had been either unitary systems or confederal systems. Power was usually exercised in a *one-way direction*. A **unitary government** is a national polity governed as a single unit. The idea is to have the central government exercising all or most political authority. A **confederation** is a group of independent states or nations that yield some of their powers to a national government. A Confederation differs from a unitary government by the way the subsidiary states much more sovereign authority. During the period of American history when the country was governed under the Articles of Confederation (1781 to 1789), the individual states had more autonomy but also less cohesion with neighboring states. Critics of that regime claimed that the absence of a weak central government left the young republic vulnerable to crises without mediation or judicial arbitration. Shay's Rebellion, a tax revolt that took place in Massachusetts, was considered the crisis that ended the United States's attempt at confederate governance.

America turned away from a unitary government style and tried a Confederation style of government for 10 years. The United States has used the federal form of governance since 1789 and the ratification of the United States Constitution. American federalism is not just the division of powers between the federal government and the states but is further nuanced by local governments. In America, the three Some of the powers that the federal government possesses it also shares with the states. These are called **concurrent powers**. Federalism is a system of implementing public policy across multiple layers of government. The process of testing and spreading ideas across multiple levels of government from federal, state, and local levels is known as diffusion. **Diffusion** is the spreading of policy ideas from one city or state to others. An example of diffusion comes whenever local governments borrow policies. If New York City were to construct an ordinance that fined litterers $100 per offense, and San Francisco copied and administered the same policy, then it was a diffusion of New York City's original concept.

4.1 The Federalist Papers and Federalism

The Federalist Papers are a collection of 85 newspaper editorials written in support of the Constitution under the pseudonym of Publius, whose real identity was three Federalists: Alexander Hamilton, James Madison, and John Jay. The word 'federalism' does not appear in the Constitution of the United States. It has been adopted and became manifest within the governmental structures as inspired by The Federalist Papers. James Madison, writing as Publius, addressed the concept of Federalism in The Federalist Papers.

There are many different topics in The Federalist Papers. In Federalist No. 39, Madison defines "republic" and establishes three rules which must apply:

1. What is the foundation of its establishment? Only the possess *ultimate* sovereignty over the government.

2. What are the sources of its power? The elected officials chosen by the people should not break the rules or abuse their power.

3. Who has the authority to make future changes? When someone is chosen to rule the country, he or she should only be in that position for a certain amount of time and must be held accountable (through impeachment if necessary) if found to have committed high crimes or treason.

The republic defined by Madison consists of the different elements of the government leadership. A Madisonian republic is a system of government as defined by these three stipulations where the citizens elect representatives to make decisions for them. This constitutes most civic officials within the three branches of government: the executive, the judicial, and the legislative. There are still some offices that are *not* directly accountable to the people. This includes justices on the Supreme Court of the United States as well as United States senators prior to the passage of the 17th Amendment. Federalists like Madison believed that there needed to be a balance of direct election (popular vote) versus internal appointment by informed elites.

Madison, along with the other framers, was aware of two methods of arranging the government: confederate or federal. The Articles of Confederation was the country's original attempt at confederacy, which was a loosely assembled body of state governments prior to the ratification of the Constitution. The second version of government is called federal, national, or consolidation. It is also known as a unitary system.

Madison's essays proposed a five-component model for the American federal system. The first component was the method of ratification. The establishment of the Constitution was not a mere proclamation or decree by central authorities. Rather it was voted upon by the various member states before becoming the supreme law of the land. The second component was the sources of power for national officers. Here Madison emphasized how the bodies of Congress (House & Senate) as well as the presidency should arise. The presidency, for example, would be subject to direct election by the people, but administered as a function of the states through the Electoral College. The third component considers the apportionment of representatives based on the census. This determines how many representatives there are per state. This third component was the establishment of the representative as a national officer. The people thus gained a national representation. The fourth component referred to a fixed number of senators; two per state. People are not represented in the Senate, the states are. The Senate reinforces the federal nature of the Constitution. Madison's fifth component was the power of the presidency. The president's power is derived from elections and governed through the Electoral College system. As was mentioned before, the popular vote of the citizens is involved with determining the president, but it is the Electoral College (based on the size of the state and its apportionment of senators and representatives) that ultimately elects the president.

4.2 Federalist Paper 10 and Factions

Federalist No. 10 was published on November 23, 1787, under the pseudonym "Publius." It addresses the question of how to reconcile citizens with interests contrary to the rights of others or the interests of the greater community. During the late 18th century, the concept of factions bothered the founding fathers. Madison saw factions within society as inevitable due to the nature of man. As long as humans hold differing opinions, have differing amounts of wealth, and own differing amounts of property, they will continue to form alliances with people who are most like them. The result is that they may work against the public interest and infringe upon the rights of others. Madison warns against these dangers.

Federalist No. 10 continues a theme begun in Federalist No. 9, "The Utility of the Union as a Safeguard Against Domestic Faction and Insurrection." Scholars and jurists contend that Federalist 9 and Federalist 10 are an authoritative interpretation and explication of the Constitution. The question of faction undergirds the development of modern interest groups and the role in which minority groups are protected from majority opinions.

In addition to the problem with factions, Federalist No. 10 continues the discussion of the question broached in Hamilton's Federalist No. 9. Hamilton there addressed the destructive role of a faction in breaking apart the republic. The role in which people form groups and allegiances dictate how effective a republic will be. The question Madison answers, then, is how to eliminate the negative effects of factions. Can a faction exist without the consequences to the republic? Madison defines a faction as many citizens, whether amounting to a minority or majority of the whole, who are united and actuated by some common impulse of passion, or of interest, adverse to the rights of other citizens, or to the permanent and aggregate interests of the community. In Madison's definition, he identifies the most serious source of faction to be the diversity of opinion in political life which leads to dispute over fundamental issues such as what regime or religion should be preferred.

Distribution of property was at the core of the debate during Madison's time. At the heart of Madison's fears about factions was the unequal distribution of property in society. The reality of property ownership was that some people owned property and others owned nothing, and Madison felt that people would form different factions that pursued different interests based on such a gap in ownership.

Recognizing that the country's wealthiest property owners formed a minority and that the country's unpropertied classes formed a majority, Madison feared that the unpropertied classes would come together to form a majority faction that gained control of the government. This fear of the minority rising became part of the framing of the American Constitution. Specifically, Madison feared that the unpropertied classes would use their majority power to implement a variety of measures that redistributed wealth in a disordered fashion. In short, Madison feared that a majority faction of the unpropertied classes might emerge to redistribute wealth and property for populist purposes and to the dismay of the ruling class, which would inevitably result in conflict.

4.3 Madison's Arguments for Faction Limitation

Madison first assessed two ways to limit the damage caused by factions: remove the causes or control the effects. He then described the two methods of removing the causes of factions: first, destroying liberty, which would work because liberty is to faction what air is to fire. The second option would be to create a society of homogeneous opinions and interests, which is difficult but not impossible. Madison particularly emphasized that economic stratification prevents everyone from sharing the same opinion. He concluded that the damage caused by factions can be limited only by controlling the effects.

Madison further contended that a person may offer two ways to check majority factions: (1) prevent the existence of the same passion or interest in a majority at the same time or, (2) render a majority faction unable to act. Madison concluded that a small democracy cannot avoid the dangers of majority faction because small size means that undesirable passions can very quickly spread to a majority of the people, which can then enact its will through the democratic government without difficulty. A republic is different from a democracy because its government is placed in the hands of delegates, and, as a result can be extended over a larger area. The idea is that, in a large republic, there will be more fit characters to choose from for each delegate.

4.4 Federalist 51 and Checks and Balances

The notion of checks and balances became fundamental in the formation of government. Federalist No. 51 is titled: "The Structure of the Government Must Furnish the Proper Checks and Balances Between the Different Departments." It was another essay by James Madison. This document was published on February 8, 1788, under the pseudonym Publius. Federalist No. 51 addresses a means by which appropriate checks and balances can be created in government and advocates a separation of powers within the national government One of its most important ideas, an explanation of check and balances, is the often-quoted phrase, "Ambition must be made to counteract ambition." In government, it is well known that people will seek to be self-promoting. Madison's idea was that the politicians and the individuals in public service in the United States would all have proclamations and ideas that they would work hard to enact-- this is true for Madison's time as well as now. The solution to ensure that laws and strong ideas were not enacted by a small group of partisan individuals was to use a federalist system where each level of government had different branches, each branch having the authority to impact the operation of the other branches. One of the primary ways that Federalist Paper 51 was able to encourage checks and balances was to tie it to the concept of liberty and an aversion to centralized tyranny. The concentration of power into one branch or level of government is antithetical to liberty. Whenever one branch or institution (of any sort) gets too much power, they become corrupted and tyrannical. As Lord Acton reminds us: "power corrupts; absolute power corrupts absolutely." Checks and balances can be a remedy to the corruption of power.

The system of checks and balances, as espoused by Madison and philosophers like John Locke and Jean-Jacques Rousseau, was designed to allow an independent function of the various branches of government within certain constraints. For example, the legislative branch would draft laws that would have to be signed (or vetoed) by the president. The Supreme Court could strike down the laws if deemed unconstitutional. The president appointed members of the court, but only by an approval vote of the Senate. It was a way to avoid allowing any one branch to gain too much influence and power.

4.5 Changes in Federalism Over Time

The balance of power between states and the national government changes over time. Because the balance of power between state and national government was clearly left open to some interpretation by the founders, it left a lot of power to the Supreme Court for interpretation. Looking at federal/state power relations over time, we can see two trends:

1. Changes like industrialization, urbanization, and advances in science and technology have led citizens to look to government at all levels for assistance, protection, and security.

2. There is an undeniable shift of power over time from the states to the national government, particularly since the culmination of the Civil War, but some of it as early as the ratification of the Constitution.

There have been some key moments where power has shifted from the states to the federal government. John Marshall's tenure as Chief Justice of the Supreme Court (1801–1835) marked a drastic shift of power from the states to the federal government. **Marshall** was the third Chief Justice of the Supreme Court. He believed in the Federalist vision of a strong national government. One of the groundbreaking cases heard under his tenure was *Marbury v. Madison*. ***Marbury v. Madison*** (1803) gave the Supreme Court the power of **judicial review** to determine if congressional laws, state laws, or executive actions are constitutional. This groundbreaking change in the role of the judiciary extended the role of checks and balances to the judicial branch with stronger enforcement.

A second key moment that shifted the power from the states to the federal government was the extension of the "Necessary and Proper Clause" in *McCulloch v. Maryland* (1819). The result of this case allowed that clause to be interpreted broadly to include many powers that were not in the Constitution.

The third key moment that shifted the power from the states to the federal governments was *Gibbons v. Ogden*. The extension of the Interstate Commerce Clause and the right to regulate commerce emanating from *Gibbons v. Ogden* (1824) opened the door to federal regulation of commerce, broadly understood to mean most forms of business. The landmark decision in which the Supreme Court of the United States held that the power to regulate interstate commerce, granted to Congress by the Commerce Clause of the United States Constitution, encompassed the power to regulate sea navigation.

4.6 Federalism: Then and Now

Nowadays, advocates of national power tend to be Democrats whose ideology leads them to believe, like the Federalists, that national power is not a threat to individual liberties. Republicans tend to be more like the Anti-Federalists in their distrust of national power and their preference for keeping important decisions at the state level. Republicans have long advocated *devolution*, or the returning of power to the states. Their enthusiasm for that position changes ~~falls~~ somewhat when they are in control of the federal government. When Republicans control Congress and the executive, many of them are less wary of the reach of the national government because it is doing their bidding. Similarly, when Democrats are out of power, they look to the states to enact their agendas. Today the battle over federalism seems to have less to do with its old framework of limited government versus big government and more to do with the battle for power between two highly polarized parties.

During the first 150 years of the United States, the country practiced something called Dual Federalism. **Dual Federalism (1789-1933)** is when you have a clear division of governing authority between national governments and state governments. One example of this is layer cake federalism, which is when you have a clear division between the authority of the state government.

During the 1930s, President Franklin D. Roosevelt's New Deal programs involved a strengthening and combination of federal/state functions. This included new regulatory agencies such as the Tennessee Valley Authority (TVA). This concept became known as Cooperative Federalism. **Cooperative Federalism (1933-1981)** is the mingling of governing authority between different levels of government.

President Ronald Reagan (1981-1989) changed how American federalism operated. It was coined **New Federalism**. **New Federalism** was a version of Cooperative Federalism but with less oversight by the federal government. It left more control to the state and local levels. New Federalism was characterized by the administering of Block Grants from the federal government to local governments. This was a way of transferring federal funds to local jurisdictions.

During the Obama administration, President Barrack Obama became known for Progressive Federalism in 2009. **Progressive Federalism** known as modern federalism is when the national government has broad goals but relies on local and state innovation to make sure they are met.

4.7 Tools Used in Modern Federalism

The modern tools used in federalism today are tied to the types of funding and programs that the federal government grants the state governments. One type of tool used by the federal government to fund state programs is a block grant. A **Block grant** gives funds that come with flexibility for the states to spend the money as they wish within broad parameters. Block grants were first introduced in 1966 as a channel for the federal government to give money to specific areas they wanted to improve. These examples in the 1960s included transportation and education. A second tool used by the federal government to fund the state governments is a categorical grant. A **categorical grant** is a grant of money with specific instructions on how it is to be spent. Finally, a third type of funding tool used by the federal government is an unfunded mandate from the federal government to the states. An **unfunded mandate** is when Congress will tell the states to do something but provide no funds for administering the policy. Unfunded mandates include local, state, and federal requirements not in synergy. For the unfunded mandate, there are federal laws or regulations that the local or state government must pay in order to enact a new law.

As one can tell, federalism has taken many shapes and forms in our country's history. There has been a general decline in the influence of the states, but the institutions of government remain similar to what was conceived by the founders of the Constitution. The United States has evolved considerably since the Articles of Confederation and the old debates over the various Federalist Papers. Things are different and they will undoubtedly change more with the passing of time. What will be the future for federalism and power sharing in America?

CHAPTER 5

The Declaration of Independence and the United States Constitution

The United States political culture resulted from the influence of English political culture and Western philosophical tradition. Since the United Colonies of America were English provinces, England has historically played an essential role in shaping American economics and culture. The ultimate political enforcer in Colonial English America was the British monarchy, which based its legitimacy on kings' divine rights. The English King was God's legitimate representative on Earth.

Since the independence period, the United States has developed a new political culture that still serves as inspiration for the rest of the world. At the time, there was no model to follow for the United States Founders. The process of writing the constitution required creativity, originality, and clarity. The Founders chose Thomas Jefferson to write the United States Declaration of Independence. The ideas of John Locke served as an inspiration to write the political document. Both legally and politically speaking, the national constitution was the founding document for the United States democracy.

5.1 The roots of the United States political culture

As a former colony, the nation was a political subject of the ruling country—England. America was economically dependent on England, and the United Colonies had cultural ties to it as well. The economic relationship between the mother country and its colonies was called *mercantilism*. England provided protection and settlement costs to the colonists. The colonies sent prime resources and cuts of the profits from their trade back to the mother country. The center of power denied colonists access to the lucrative markets in which England competed.

The ultimate political enforcer in Colonial English America was the British monarchy. England followed the *divine right of kings*, which had its roots in a political culture that understood the power to be vested in the king because he was God's legitimate representative on Earth. This situation put a significant burden on the colonists to produce a counternarrative to justify political independence that did not make them all sinners. As the American colonists began to consider themselves a separate cultural and political entity, the idea of struggling for independence started to look like a desirable and viable option for some American-born Englishmen.

More than anything, the Americans developed a new way of looking at the world during the independence days. The social contract theory was essential to the development of the United States as an independent country. This theory principally emerged and took shape from the writings of the British philosophers Thomas Hobbes and John Locke. In a *social contract*, power is to be held by all citizens, each of whom gives up some of their rights to the government in exchange for the right to use safely and securely the power citizens retained.

The recently-formed government based its legitimacy on the consent of those governed. If the government did not adequately protect and guarantee their remaining rights, subjects had the right to rebel and establish a new government. A government that does not secure the remaining rights of citizens lacks legitimacy.

British political philosopher Thomas Hobbes believed that free men had the right to subject themselves to a ruler who would protect them. The government was an all-powerful entity, and its subjects had no right to push back against its power. On the other hand, John Locke believed that the social contract was conditional upon rights' protection. Governed subjects could revoke the social contract if the government failed to safeguard their rights.

Of all the political thinkers who influenced American beliefs about government, the most relevant was assuredly John Locke, who wrote nearby in time that the founders of the United States were contemplating independence. The ideas of Locke were hugely popular in the United Colonies of America. When discussing the influences of the political philosophy of John Locke, one should start by analyzing and focusing on the theory of natural law and rights. However, one should consider that the natural law concept existed long before Locke and was an integral principle of his philosophical theories. The natural law is a way to express universal moral truths that apply to all people. Universal moral law likely served as a preceding influence of the United States Constitution.

In many more than one pamphlet, the United States writers and thinkers cited Locke on natural rights and the social and governmental contract as well; they referred to Montesquieu and Delolme on the character of British freedom and the institutional prerequisites for its fulfillment; Voltaire on the evils and disasters of clerical oppression; Beccaria on the change of criminal law; Grotius, Pufendorf, Burlamaqui; and Vattel on the laws of nature and nations, and the standards of civil government. The pervasiveness of such citations is, on occasion, astonishing.[48]

The most significant early contrast was between natural and generally applicable laws and those conventional, which operated only in those places where specific particular customs existed. Simply put, this is a contrast between a universal moral right and a law created by society

---

[48] Bailyn, Bernard. *The Ideological Origins of the American Revolution*, 1967. Massachusetts: Belknap Press.

depending on culture and historical tradition. This distinction is known as one of the main differences between natural law and positive law.

Natural law also differs from divine law. Divine law is from the Christian tradition and customarily referred to those laws that God had directly revealed through visionary prophets and other enlightened writers. One can discover natural law by reason alone. Natural law applies to all people. On the contrary, one can get in touch with divine law only through God's special revelation, and it is only applicable to those whom the revelation God disclosed. For Locke, the biblical law did not apply to the modern human being[49].

5.2 The Declaration of Independence

The Founders chose Thomas Jefferson to write the *Declaration of Independence*. The ideas of John Locke served as an inspiration to write the document. Locke, born in 1632, is among the most influential political philosophers in history. In the *Two Treatises of Government*, Locke supported the claim that men are by nature free and equal against those that said that God had made all people naturally subject to a divinely-legitimate monarch. He argued that humans have natural rights, such as the right to life, liberty, and property.

The rights to life, liberty, and property are universal and natural. These rights have a foundation independent of the cultural and consuetudinary law built on any particular society's traditions. Locke stated that all men are naturally free and equal as part of the justification for understanding the legitimate political government that results from the social contract. This social contract is a condition in which people in the state of nature conditionally transfer some of their rights to the government, which subjects expect to provide stable and comfortable enjoyment of their lives, liberty, and property.

---

[49] For an in-depth analysis of Locke's influence in United States independence, see Bailyn.

The Declaration of Independence is a political document about changing the rules about what makes power legitimate and who should reasonably hold it. The historical record represents the social contract between the government and the U.S. people. By relying on the social contract, the Declaration of Independence stated that Americans had *inalienable rights* that subjects could not give up to the government.

One should acknowledge that the American Constitution created the modern notion of citizens distinct from subjects. Even if related, both terms are not equivalent. The United States constitution writers laid blame on George III for breaking a political contract he barely understood. This incident was one of the main circumstances that legitimated the Americans' rebellion. It also attempted to convince the leaders of other colonial powers like Spain and France that they had nothing to worry about since supposedly they were not tyrants like George, King of Great Britain, and Ireland. Not every person in the new country was a citizen with full political rights. The task of creating a new government was not as easy as they had hoped, and it took more than one try to get things done right.

5.3 The United States Constitution

The constitution is the framework for the legal system of the United States. Depending upon the constitution's definition and since some Nation-States do not have a formal central constitution like the United States, one can argue that the United States Constitution is the oldest codified constitutional text still in use today. The United States Constitution is divided into Articles and Amendments. Congress Representatives have updated the American Constitution over the years, and courts continue to argue the text's applications. Both legally and politically speaking, the national constitution was the founding document for the United States democracy.

The Preamble of the United States Constitution—the document's famous first fifty-two words— introduces everything to follow in the

Constitution's seven articles and twenty-seven amendments. It proclaims who is adopting this Constitution: "We the People of the United States." It describes why the country adopts the Constitution—the purposes behind the enactment of America's governing charter. Furthermore, it explains the principles adopted, as the United Constitution, a single authoritative written text, serves as the land's fundamental law.

While accurate, the word "preamble" does not quite capture the full importance of this provision. "Preamble" implies that these words are merely an opening rhetorical flourish or frill without meaningful effect. To be sure, "preamble" usefully conveys the idea that this provision does not itself confer or delineate powers of government or rights of citizens, outlined in the substantive articles and amendments that follow in the main body of the constitution's text.

5.4 The Articles of Confederation

Before the Civil War, the two leading and legislative power-affecting doctrines of American Constitutional Law were the Doctrine of Vested Rights and the Police Power Doctrine, both complementary to each other. The first one presumably flourished before the rise of the Jacksonian Democracy style in the United States. The Doctrine of the Vested Rights is the more fundamental doctrine[50].

The United States Constitution has a foundation in the Articles of Confederation. The founders' primary duty was to write a constitution or political rulebook that would determine who would have power, how that power would be limited, and how the new government functioned. The first constitution has been historically known as the *Articles of Confederation*. Because the states viewed themselves as sovereign, they decided to limit their new constitution to a "firm league of friendship" amongst states rather than a complete union entity. This change was

---

[50] Corwin, Edward. "The Basic Doctrine of American Constitutional Law." *Michigan Law Review*, vol. 12, no. 4, 1914, pp. 247–276. *JSTOR*, www.jstor.org/stable/1276027.

about the establishment of a *United States Confederation.* Economic troubles, drought, and crop failures meant that there were heavy demands for relief from state governments.

The Articles of Confederation provided new restrictions on the government's power. The national government was not allowed to take some measures under the Articles of Confederation, such as draft soldiers' power. Drafting soldiers allowed for a robust military force; whoever, not allowing a draft made it challenging to coordinate a response to a threat from a foreign power. The Articles of Confederation stopped citizens' taxation, making the Federal government dependent on the states for funds. The Articles could not regulate interstate commerce; consequently, it left the states to create their own markets, economic rules, and more. Furthermore, the Articles forbid establishing a central monetary system and having different currencies in each state.

The last draft of the Articles of Confederation, which framed the new country's government's basis, was acknowledged by Congress in November 1777 and submitted to the states for endorsement. It would not become the tradition that must be adhered to until every one of the thirteen states had endorsed it. Within two years, all except for Maryland had done so. Maryland contended that all domains west of the Appalachians, to which a few states had laid case, should instead be held by the public government as open land to help every state. When the remainder of these states, Virginia, surrendered its property claims in mid-1781, Maryland affirmed the Confederation Articles. Half a month later, the British capitulated. Americans aspired their new government to be a republic, wherein people, not a monarch or ruler, held power and chose agents to oversee as per law and order.

Many feared that a country as large as the United States would not be managed successfully as a republic. Those voices also stressed that even an administration of delegates elected by the people might become too powerful and overbearing. Subsequently, public administrators created a confederation as an entity in which independent, self-governing states form a union to act together in defense areas. Unfortunate of supplanting one abusive public government with another. Nonetheless, the Articles of Confederation's composers made collusion of sovereign states held together by a feeble focal government.[51]

The result of the problems with the Articles led to economic problems. When economic chaos arose, so did Shay's Rebellion. Shay's Rebellion was a march of angry farmers demanding debt relief in western Massachusetts. This rebellion drove some of the founders to meet in Annapolis in 1786 to discuss fixing the dysfunctional Articles. Later, some at the gathering in Annapolis decided the Articles were too broken to fix, and thus they decided to create a whole new Constitution instead.

5.5 The Constitutional Convention

The drafting of a new national constitution began with the Constitutional Convention of 1787. The most significant fracture came between two groups, the first known as the Federalists and the second as the Anti-Federalists. The Federalists were those who wanted a more robust national government. The prospect of a stronger government less threatened the Federalists because they mainly were representatives of large states who felt they could control national government power. Over time, they were known as the Federalists because they preferred to get rid of the Articles' confederal system, where the states ultimately held power and moved to a federal system, where power would be shared between states and national government.

There were multiple plans put forth at the Constitutional Convention as proposals for the new government. One plan put forward was a bicameral legislature by Virginia. The *Virginia Plan* was a comparatively strong but limited government whose signature institution would be a *bicameral legislature* (meaning it would have two chambers). The representation in both chambers would be based on population and taxes paid. On the other hand, the Anti-Federalists were against a robust

[51] Corwin, 33-44.

national government on principle and out of fear. They would have preferred to tweak the Articles to make them more valuable and practical. Mostly, representatives of smaller states feared a more robust government would roll over them, and the big states would always get their way. The *New Jersey Plan* wanted a slightly upgraded Articles of Confederation—a single chamber of the legislature where every state cast one vote, with a weak executive and a nonexistent court system, but some additional powers for the national government.

The solution to this political crisis was the agreements on compromises. The **Great Compromise** was "great" because it effectively worked to bring the two sides together. However, it was more remarkable for the Federalists than the Anti-Federalists since the outcome exceeded its initial expectations. The Federalists truly benefited from the negotiation results. The Compromise the two groups agreed on called for a bicameral legislature that split the difference between the two political sides. Parliamentary representation was based on the state's population in the House of Representatives. Every state received two members, regardless of population, in the Senate.

The result of the Great Compromise was the *Three-Fifths Compromise* indicates that, when determining representation, the population count would be made "by adding to the whole Number of Free persons ... three-fifths of all other persons." Both the Great Compromise and the Three-Fifths Compromise reduced the national government's popular control by countering it with state control and significantly empowering smaller, rural states.

The concerns of southern states to boost their power vis-a-vis the north had another lasting effect on the United States Constitution: we do not elect the United States president by direct popular vote. Instead, we have the Electoral College. In this settlement, the states had more power to choose the president. The number of electors a state gets in the Electoral College (that is, the number of votes that a state can cast for president) is determined by the total number of representatives that that state has in both houses. The South fought a direct popular presidential election because actual population totals would have determined the presidency in some cases.

5.6 Basic Constitutional Principles

The American founders had created a document that was path-breaking in its innovative approach to human governance. Several nations have throughout the years used the United States Constitution as an inspiration, but at the time, there was no model for the American founders to follow. The writers of the national constitution were original and have inspired other states throughout history. *James Madison* was the genius behind the United States Constitution. His fundamental idea was to design a system that takes human nature *as it is* (self-interested, greedy, and ambitious), not as you want it to be. James Madison wanted to create an internal mechanism based on the idea that human nature will produce fair laws and public policy because of it, not despite it.

Basic principles of the United States provided by the national constitution are to have separation of powers[52], checks and balances, and federalism. The United States Constitution gives the three branches of government their own powers, shared powers, and checked powers. In some countries, these functions are not separated (i.e., a *parliamentary system*).

Separation of powers is the government's division vertically into three branches: legislative, executive, and judicial. This power division gives each layer and branch independent status with some of its constitutional power.

The founders thought a presidential system would better protect against abuses of power. In the United States, we have a *presidential system*: the executive and the other two branches are constitutionally distinct. The three are given their own powers according to the United States Constitution. *Checks and balances* give each layer and branch just enough

---

[52] On the separation of powers in the United States constitution, see Corwin.

power over the others in its system that their jealousy will guard against the others' over-reach. Simply put, the *legislative branch* is the lawmaking component, the *executive branch* is the law-enforcing component, and the *judicial branch* is the law-interpreting component. *Federalism* divides the government horizontally into layers: national and state.

5.7 Constitutional Powers

The United States Constitution provides powers to the Federal government and the states. The constitutional provisions fostered federalism's development. Article I Section 8 (*enumerated powers*) spells out exactly what Congress (and hence the national government) is allowed to do, including coining money and managing interstate commerce.

The *necessary and proper clause* coming at the end of the enumerated powers indicates Congress can do anything "necessary and proper" to carry out its duties suitably. The United States constitution's necessary and proper clause defines the Congress's authority to exercise the necessary and proper powers it needs to carry out its designated functions. This power or clause of the United States Constitution also goes by a similar name, *the elastic clause,* because it stretches the national government's authority to include or imply anything written in the United States Constitution's text. In practice, this clause generally strengthens the national government at the expense of state power.

The *Tenth Amendment to the United States Constitution* indicates that any powers not explicitly given to the national government are reserved to the states. It ultimately depends on what the Court says, and the Court changes its mind repeatedly. Who gets the advantage? It is pretty much a tie; the balance of national state power again depends on judicial interpretation.

In Article VI of the Constitution, the *supremacy clause* states that the constitutional text itself and national laws made under it are the land's law. This clause found in the Constitution defines the national government's authority. The supremacy clause says that the national government's authority prevails over state or local government claims provided that power was given to the federal government. This idea found in the United States Constitution provides the federal government's implied powers, and when laws between States and Federal governments clash, the Federal Government's laws are supreme and take priority over the state's laws. Who gets the advantage? If national law clashes with state law, national law almost always wins if the federal government chooses to impose its will.

The founders were well aware of the tension between the states themselves as a threat to national stability. The United States Constitution's framers developed a formal way to balance federal vs. state rights. The *Constitution's full faith and credit clause* (Article IV, Section 1) says that the states have to respect the other states' legal proceedings and public acts. An example of the full faith and credit clause includes one's driver's license, which must be accepted across state lines as a valid form of identification. The *privileges and immunities clause* (Article IV, Section 2) indicates a state cannot deny a citizen of another state the rights its citizens enjoy.

The balance has changed over time, but the national government has often gained power at the states' expense. Battles over federalism are typically fought in the states, except for the Civil War. The history of federalism proves that national and state governments have periodically checked each other over time.

CHAPTER 6

Civil Liberties

6.1 Introduction to Civil Liberties

What is the difference between civil rights and civil liberties? It is the word *civil*—having to do with the nonpolitical life of citizens—that gives the phrases *civil rights* and *civil liberties* specific and different meanings. In democracies and other non-authoritarian societies where, at least some political power is held by citizens, both civil liberties and civil rights are essential to operational societies. Civil liberties are individual rights that come from the *limitation of* government power. Civil rights *empower the government* to give us group rights. You could say civil liberties are about equal protection *from* the law and civil rights are about the equal protection *of* the laws.

So, what do civil liberties and civil rights actually mean in order to differentiate from one another? **Civil liberties** are the individual freedoms that limit government. These rights are guaranteed by the Bill of Rights and the text of the Constitution itself. Some others, like the right to privacy, come from Supreme Court decisions that have interpreted the Constitution. **Civil rights** are the freedom of groups to fully participate in the public life of a nation. These groups are defined by some particular characteristic—like race, gender, or sexual orientation—that is beyond their members' control. Rather than limiting government, the protection of civil rights often *empowers the government* to act.

6.2 Rights Equal Power

Giving citizenry rights empowers the people. Rights confer power on people and limitations on government. When a person has the ability to claim a right, it makes one a citizen, not a subject. The ability to deny rights gives citizens power over each other. The ability to use government to fight back against those who would deny their fellow citizens rights is also a form of power.

6.3 Where do our rights come from?

If we believe we have rights because the government, the Constitution, the Bill of Rights or any other amendments grant them to us, then those rights can also be taken away. These rights differ from **natural rights**, which are the inalienable rights conferred by "Nature and Nature's God" that no government can take away.

The rights of American citizens provided by the Constitution and the Bill of Rights are limited in two main ways. First, they become limited when they clash with other people's rights. Second, is when they conflict with collective societal values. Solving rights conflicts often involve compromise. These conflicts are resolved by different aspects of government such as Congress, the President and the bureaucracy, the courts, and the people.

6.4 The Bill of Rights

The Bill of Rights established the fundamental constitutional rights afforded to every American. These important rights are included in the Bill of Rights. These rights are:

- Amendment 1: Establishment clause, free exercise of religion, free speech, free press, right to assemble.
- Amendment 2: Right to bear arms necessary for a well-regulated militia.

- Amendment 3: You can't be forced to house soldiers during peace.
- Amendment 4: No unreasonable searches and seizures.
- Amendment 5: Grand jury indictment for capital crimes; no double jeopardy, self-incrimination, or deprivation of property without due process of law.
- Amendment 6: Right to a speedy trial and counsel.
- Amendment 7: Jury trials for civil cases where the value in controversy is over $20.
- Amendment 8: No cruel or unusual punishment or excessive bail.
- Amendment 9: The rights listed in the Constitution does not limit the possession of other rights.
- Amendment 10: All rights not given to the national government are reserved to the states.

The founders struggled with having a Bill of Rights. Alexander Hamilton argued in *Federalist* #84 that a Bill of Rights might be redundant, because the founders' intent was to create a government that was already powerless to do the things the Bill of Rights ruled out. All of the founders feared a powerful government; they just differed on ways to limit it. The Federalists thought they had created internal mechanisms—separation of powers, checks and balances—that would keep the government from over-reaching. The Anti-Federalists wanted to spell out restrictions on the government—limiting powers the Federalists didn't think the Constitution conferred.

The Bill of Rights limited the national government's power. On its face, the Bill of Rights applies to the national government and specifically to Congress. But most Americans don't interact with the federal government or commit federal crimes. States may have their own Bill of Rights within their own state constitutions, but states are not required to guarantee these rights and there are no regulations about what their state constitutions should cover.

The power of the states is checked or held accountable by the federal government. Americans are not helpless if a state denies them a basic right. **The Fourteenth Amendment** was originally drafted and intended to stop southern states from denying former slaves their citizenship rights after the Civil War. Using a process called **incorporation**, the Court was able to fold the national right into required state protections via the Fourteenth Amendment. Language in the Fourteenth Amendment can be interpreted to mean that no state can deny a citizen any of the rights the federal government guarantees. With incorporation, the Supreme Court expanded the national power at the expense of the state, changing the balance of federal power.

6.5 Civil Liberties—Understanding the First Amendment

The basic civil liberties of Americans include all the rights the founders felt were necessary to keep the states in check. The most important of those rights they packed into the First Amendment, because they wanted to indicate their primary importance. The reason that this amendment covers so many rights is that, for the founders, these were all fundamental to a fully functioning democracy.

The First Amendment prohibits Congress from establishing a religion or interfering with the exercise of religion, abridging the freedom of speech or the press, or interfering with the right of the people to assemble. These prohibitions have been made applicable to the states through the Fourteenth Amendment. The freedoms, however, are not absolute and encompass different boundaries that have been established by judicial interpretation.

6.6 Freedom of Religion.

Freedom of religion was important to the founders. The founders' main task was to write a constitution, or rulebook, that would determine how the new government was to function, who would have power, and how that power would be limited. The Articles of Confederation gave the foundational importance to the writing of the Bill of Rights because religious freedom was at the forefront of the founders' minds. Many of the original colonists had fled England to avoid an established church in the first place.

The First Amendment has two clauses that establish freedom of religion. The First Amendment provides "Congress shall make no law respecting an establishment of religion or prohibiting the free exercise thereof".

Establishment Clause

First, the **Establishment Clause** was designed to limit Congress and ensure that Congress shall make no law respecting an establishment of religion. The role of the state is to accommodate all religions. Unfortunately, this first amendment guarantee can be divisive. **Accommodationists** are people who want to support "all" religions equally. This is opposed to **separationists**: people who want a separation between church and state. Americans and, indeed, members of the Supreme Court, are divided on whether we need to keep church and state entirely separate, or whether it is okay to allow some state recognition and support for religion as long as it accommodates all religions. What is a constitutional issue—how far church and state can be intermingled—has become a cultural clash that it is almost impossible to solve to everyone's satisfaction.

The first step is to determine if the law has a religious preference. When determining if a law or government program violates the Establishment Clause and includes a preference for some religious sects over others, the law or program will be subject to a compelling interest analysis and ask if it is **narrowly tailored** to promote a **compelling interest**. In *Board of Education v. Grumet*, the Supreme Court struck down a state law that created a public school district whose boundaries were intentionally set to match the boundaries of a particular Jewish neighborhood. Since the government had no other interest rather than one that was furthered by "religious favoritism", the Court held it failed to exercise governmental authority in a religiously neutral way.[53] Therefore, if there is a preference and the law is not crafted in a religiously neutral way, it will receive the compelling interest test.

Secondly, if there is no religious preference, and the compelling interest test is not used, then the law is subject to the Lemon Test. The **Lemon Test** was established in *Lemon v. Kurtzman* to provide a constitutional understanding on how much the government can establish a religion. The law or program will be valid under the Establishment Clause if it:

1. Has a **secular** purpose

2. Has a **primary effect** that neither **advances** nor **inhibits** religion; and

3. Does not produce excessive government **entanglement** with religion.[54]

"Secular", as opposed to sacred, means not having a religious, spiritual or temporal basis. If the government maintains a holiday-Christmas Times display that does not appear to endorse one religion and includes holiday decorations, such as a Christmas tree or a Santa Claus figure, the court will hold that the display has a **secular purpose** based on the history of government recognition of holidays.[55]

If the law **advances** or **inhibits** a particular religion or specific religious group, then that law will be invalid. But if a law favors or burdens a larger segment of society that happens to include religious groups, it will generally be upheld. For example, the IRS may provide deductions and other financial benefits to churches and other religious donations because the **primary effect** of the benefit does not only include religious

[53] *Board of Education v. Grumet*, 512 v. 687 (1994).
[54] *Lemon v. Kurtzman*, 403 U.S. 602 (1971).
[55] *County of Allegheny v. ACLU*, 492 U.S. 573 (1989).

organizations- but it also applies to all charitable organizations that happen to include religious groups.[56]

It is hard for the Court to decide what "excessive entanglement" means. **Excessive entanglement** can mean too much government involvement. There are times when government action can cross paths with private religions. It becomes excessive when government action crosses into religious action that they can run afoul of other people's actions or the state's obligation to exercise its police power to protect the health, well-being, and security of all citizens. For example, if a public school allows members of the public and private organizations to use school property when classes are not in session and a religious organization utilizes the space and the meetings are not run by school personnel, there is no excessive government entanglement.[57] The government was not a significant actor.

Free Exercise Clause

The freedom from an establishment of a religion afforded the free exercise of religion for the founders. Because the government cannot establish one or more religions means people have the freedom to practice any religion. The **Free Exercise Clause** states that Congress shall make no law... prohibiting the free exercise thereof.[58] The trouble with those words spelling out religious freedom protection is that they contain an inherent contradiction. Any effort to establish one of the founders' denominations as the official state religion would have doomed the new country from the start. When political differences are reinforced with religious differences, every conflict is infused with profound meaning and compromise is impossible. When a government can put the power of an Almighty behind its laws, it is very hard to resist it if it over-reaches.

---

[56] *Hernandez v. Commissioner of Internal Revenue*, 490 U.S. 680 (1989).
[57] *Good News Club v. Milford Central School*, 533 U.S. (2001).
[58] U.S. Const. Amend I.

The Free Exercise Clause prohibits the government from punishing, denying benefits to or imposing burdens on someone on the basis of the person's religious beliefs. For many years the Supreme Court had suggested that the government had to show it had a compelling reason to infringe on religious practice. But in 1990 it reversed course and put the burden of proof back on religious groups to show that the state regulation has violated the groups' rights. However, the test for such impermissible government action remains unclear as the Court has never found an interest that was so compelling that it would justify punishing or regulating a religious belief.

The Court has directed that the Free Exercise Clause prohibits the government from punishing conduct merely because it is religious or displays religious belief.[59] A law that is designed to suppress actions only because the actions are religiously motivated is not a neutral law and would be invalid. A city law that prohibits a precise type of animal slaughtering for a particular religion violates the Free Exercise clause because the law was not neutral and did not prohibit all animal slaughtering.[60]

But the states can prohibit or regulate conduct in general, and this is true even if the prohibition or regulation happens to interfere with a person's religious practices. The Free Exercise Clause does not require exemptions from criminal laws or other regulations. A law that regulates conduct of all persons can be applied to prohibit the conduct of a person despite the fact that his or her religious beliefs prevent him or her from complying with the law. For example, the prohibition against the use of peyote was permissible if it applied generally to all persons, even if individuals require use of peyote during religious ceremonies.[61]

But what is a religious belief?

The Supreme Court has not defined or laid out elements for what constitutes a religious belief. However, it has made clear that religious beliefs

---

[59] *Employment Division v. Smith.*

[60] *Church of the Lukumi v. Babalu Aye, Inc. v. Hialeah*, 508 U.S. 520 (1993).

[61] *Employment Division v. Smith.*

do not require recognition of a supreme being[62] and need not arise from a traditional, or even an organized, religion.[63]

6.7 Why freedom of expression is a BIG deal

As important to the founders in limiting government as freedom from an established religion was **freedom of expression**. Freedom of expression includes speech, press, and **freedom of assembly**, the right to join together with other persons for expressive or political activity. While freedom of speech and press are mentioned in the First Amendment, freedom of association is not mentioned but is still protected by the First Amendment. The freedom of speech protects the free flow of ideas, a most important function in a democratic society. A regulation or law that tries to forbid speech of specific ideas (**content regulation**) is more likely to violate the free speech doctrine. It is usually unconstitutional for the government to prohibit speech based on its content. In ***Brandenburg v. Ohio***, the Court held that the government could not prohibit political speech, or speech with political content, unless it is linked to immediate lawless behavior[64]. However, **conduct regulation**, which is content-neutral and regulates how the speech is conducted, is more likely permitted (*i.e.*, law prohibiting billboards for purposes of traffic safety).

Speech and communication, and its conduct from which it is expressed, can take many forms and, if that conduct is intended to express an idea, can still be protected under the First Amendment much like content speech. In *Masterpiece Cakeshop v. Colorado Civil Rights Commission*, a cake shop owner refused to sell a wedding cake to a same sex couple, claiming, in part, requiring him to create the cake would violate his First Amendment right to free speech by compelling him to exercise his artistic talents to express a message with which he disagreed.

---

[62] *Torcaso v. Watkins*, 367 U.S. 488 (1961).

[63] *Frazee v. Illinois Department of Employment Security*, 489 U.S. 829 (1989).

[64] *Brandenburg v. Ohio*, 395 U.S. 444 (1969)

The Court did not rule on the speech claim but agreed with the Court of Appeals holding that preparing a wedding cake is not a form of protected speech or would force the cake shop owner to adhere to and express an ideological point of view. In their concurring opinion, Justices Kagen and Breyer, note and insinuate that cake making is certainly a conduct for which speech is expressed, which is generally permitted. However, the Justices noted that "the Court has recognized a wide array of conduct that can qualify as expressive, including nude dancing, wearing a military uniform and conducting a silent sit-in" and cake making also be a type of protected speech conduct if it intends to express an idea. Here the Justices suggest that conduct, like making a cake, can be protected speech if the cake maker uses his artistic talent of cake making as an expression of value, or opinion. [65]

Freedom of expression is important predominantly for the right to criticize the government. Denying free speech sets a dangerous precedent—if we can stop our opponents from speaking out today, they might stop us from speaking out tomorrow. So, if free speech is so important, why do we ever limit it?

The Supreme Court has at various times ruled that speech (and symbolic speech) can be limited. As indicated above, very few restrictions on the content of speech are tolerated. The Court allows them only to prevent grave injury. The following is a list of the reasons for which the Court has allowed content-based restrictions on speech:

- For purposes of national security during war (**sedition**)
- Because it is **obscene**
- Speech that is inherently likely to incite immediate physical retaliation (**fighting words**)
- Because it maliciously damages a reputation (**libel** when printed; **slander** when spoken)

---

[65] *Masterpiece Cakeshop v. Colorado Civil Rights Commission*, 138 S. Ct. 1719 (2018).

To determine what is unprotected speech, the Court has come up with a series of tests, many of which have introduced even more ambiguity. The **clear and present danger test** was meant to distinguish speech that was immediately harmful from that posed only a remote threat.[66] The **imminent lawless action test** protected speech unless it was directed to producing or inciting imminent lawless action and is likely to produce or incite such action.[67] The *Miller* **test** defines standards for obscenity and asks whether the work lacks "serious literary, artistic, political, or scientific value".[68] The **prior restraint test** prohibits censoring and refusing to allow the publication of something, even though it very well might fail one of its tests after publication. The Supreme Court has been fairly steady on its refusal to engage in prior restraint.[69] Only a national emergency could justify such censorship.

6.8 Electronic communication makes it vastly more complicated.

In addition to the wide variety of types of speech discussed above, electronic communication can also be a type of speech. The question as to whether media companies can limit access to the internet is evolving. The role of **net neutrality** is the way the Internet works now on the principle that service providers cannot speed up or slow down access for customers or make decisions about the content they see or the apps they download. The Supreme Court is constantly, and likely indefinitely, interpreting the Free Speech Clause to keep up with new types of speech created through new technology.

---

[66] *Scheneck v. United States*, 249 U.S. 47 (1919).
[67] *Brandenberg v. Ohio*, 395 U.S. 444 (1969).
[68] *Miller v. California*, 413 U.S. 15 (1973).
[69] *Near v. Minnesota*, 283 U.S. 697 (1931)

6.9 Civil Liberties—Understanding Due Process Rights

What are due process rights? **Due process rights** are the rights that give Americans some protections against being railroaded into jail by the police and the courts, especially for political purposes. The founders devote half the Bill of Rights to this subject to protect the citizens from a police state. A chief fear of the founders was a government so strong that its leaders could use the police power and the judicial system for political purposes. These protections provide that the government shall not take a person's life, liberty, or property without due process of law. Due process contemplates fair procedures, which at least require at least an opportunity to present objections to the proposed action to a fair, neutral decision maker, like a judge. There are two separate clauses protecting due process: (1) The Due Process Clause in the Fifth Amendment (applies to the federal government) and (2) The Due Process Clause in the Fourteenth Amendment (applies to state and local governments).

6.10 What do the due process rights include?

Article I provides that Congress cannot suspend habeas corpus, pass a bill of attainder, and pass an ex post facto law. Congress cannot suspend a person's right to be brought before a judge. The writ of **habeas corpus** is the right from unlawful imprisonment and includes the right to be brought before a judge and informed of the charges and evidence against you. The due process rights of people cannot be violated by acts of Congress unduly targeting them by passing a bill of attainer. A **bill of attainder** is a law directed at an individual or group that accuses and convicts them without a trial. The due process of people is so important that Congress was precluded from making laws to incriminate people for actions previously committed. An **ex post facto law** is a law that makes a criminal act (not civil regulation, such as denial of a professional license) illegal that was innocent when done, or "after the fact", hereby not allowing an accused to make an informed decision about the legality of his or her actions before he or she acts.[70] The right to be brought before a judge, informed of the law and charges and receiving a trial, ensures a due or appropriate judicial process before a conviction.

Due process rights include civil liberties. The **exclusionary rule** prohibits evidence from being introduced at a criminal trial if it was obtained by violating your civil liberties protected under the Constitution. The main purpose of the exclusionary rule is to deter the government, usually the police, from violating a person's civil liberties and constitutional rights. If the government cannot use evidence obtained in violation of a person's rights, it will be less likely to infringe on the person's rights.

The right to self-protection in a police arrest is guaranteed under the Fifth Amendment which provides that no person "shall be compelled to be a witness against himself...".[71] This has been interpreted to establish a guarantee against compelled incrimination. *Miranda* **rights** come from the case that established that you have the right to be told that you possess these rights and guarantees.[72] Miranda rights are a set of warnings that must be given to an accused person that is in custody prior to any police interrogation. In order for the accused statement's to be later admissible in court, the accused must be clearly informed that: (1) he or she has the right to remain silent, (2) anything he or she says can be used against him in court, (3) he or she has the right to an attorney, and (4) if he or she cannot afford an attorney, one will be appointed.

While the above are some examples, additional civil rights and liberties include a right to be told why you are being arrested, a right to not be tried twice for the same crime, a right to an attorney and the right to resist questioning.

---

[70] U.S. Const. Art. I §9 prohibits the federal government and U.S. Const. Art. I §10 prohibits the states from passing ex post facto laws.

[71] U.S. Const. Amend. V.

[72] *Miranda v. Arizona*, 384 U.S. 436 (1966).

6.11 Civil Liberties—Understanding the Right to Privacy

What is the right to privacy? While one can argue that the founders created a limited government and never intended it to be powerful enough to infringe on the private lives of Americans, none of them thought it a serious enough threat to put it into the document itself. The right to privacy is a judicial creation of the Supreme Court in the 1965 case of *Griswold v. Connecticut.*[73] In this case the Court declared that the Constitution does guarantee a "zone of privacy" within a "penumbra" of existing fundamental constitutional guarantees and amendments. Since there was no actual right to privacy mentioned in the Constitution or any of the amendments, the justices "found" such a right to be implied in the Bill of Rights. These specific rights for privacy emanated from:

- The First Amendment protection of one's beliefs and speech
- The Fourth Amendment protection against unreasonable searches and seizures
- The Fifth Amendment protection against self-incrimination
- The Ninth Amendment's promise that one's rights weren't limited to the ones enumerated in the document

The Supreme Court extended this right to privacy marriage, sexual relations, abortion, childrearing and LGTBQ rights in later decisions. The right to privacy has become controversial because, through constant interpretation of the Constitution, the Court creates new rights not explicit in the Constitution. The disagreement arises because the precedent set in *Griswold* was the basis for the landmark, and most controversial, decision in *Roe v. Wade*, which held the right to privacy includes the right to abortion with some limitations.[74] Although contraception may not be all that controversial when considered today (unless we are talking about

---

[73] *Griswold v. Connecticut*, 381 U.S. 479 (1965).
[74] *Roe v. Wade, 410 U.S. 113* (1973).

the provision of health care), abortion still definitely is decades after the *Roe* decision.

The conflict over the right to privacy brings us back to Hamilton's *Federalist* #84. Underlying this controversy is an interesting constitutional issue: whether the Constitution should be read literally as the founders wrote it or whether it can be read flexibly in the light of contemporary circumstances. The first position is exactly the argument that Hamilton feared would be made if a Bill of Rights were to be attached to the Constitution. The right to privacy has become a target of those who argue that position.

The method in which the court systems interpret the Constitution can be either strict constructionists or judicial interpretivists. **Strict constructionists** are scholars and judges who believe that the Constitution should be read just as it was written. **Judicial interpretivists** are those who believe that the founders could not have anticipated all the changes that make the world today different from theirs and, therefore, that judges should read the Constitution as the founders would write it in light of modern-day experience. Strict constructionists generally interpret the Constitution to limit rights to privacy, while judicial interpretivists recognize the evolving right to privacy as implied in the Constitution.

The method in which a justice interprets the Constitution determines how rights are created from the constitution. The political significance of this argument today can give people new civil rights and liberties or take them away. Since individual interpretations of the Constitution have such clear policy implications, Supreme Court confirmation hearings have often become battlegrounds as well. Reproductive rights are not the only ones that fall under the right to privacy. Supporters of LGBTQ rights tried to use the right to privacy to fight laws that criminalized homosexual behavior but were initially unsuccessful. Slowly, the Court recognized the LGBT community has some protections under the right to privacy by holding unmarried couples (largely LGBTQ couples since same sex marriage was illegal at the time) had the same right to obtain contraception as married couples.[75] The movement has had setbacks in 1986 when the Court held that the Constitutional guarantees don't prohibit states from criminalizing sex between people of the same sex. In *Bowers v. Hardwick*, the Court held that the right of privacy recognized in cases such as *Griswold* and *Roe* does not prevent the criminalization of homosexual conduct between consenting adults. [76] The opinion of the Supreme Court pendulum swung again in 2003 and reversed their prior decision and held that the due process clause gave people "the full right to engage in private conduct without government intervention...[and there is] no legitimate state interest which can justify its intrusion into the individual's personal and private life."[77]

A landmark decision in 2015 held that the fundamental right to marry under the right to privacy is guaranteed to same-sex couples in *Obergefell v. Hodges*.[78] While the law is slowly moving in the direction to eventually provide full equal protection for the LGTBQ community, it is likely that real change will be incremental, and the movement has a long way to go.

---

[75] *Eisenstadt v. Baird*, 405 U.S. 438 (1972).
[76] *Bowers v. Hardwick*, 478 U.S. 186 (1986).
[77] *Lawrence v. Texas*, 539 U.S. 558 (2003).
[78] *Obergefell v. Hodges*, 576 U.S. 644 (2015)

CHAPTER 7

Civil Rights in America

Chapter summary

Not all people have always had equality under the law in the United States of America. The dilemma of equal protection is vital to ensure that some people in America do not have more rights afforded them than others. Discrimination occurs when the government treats its citizens differently and usually takes the form of denying a benefit or imposing a burden or penalty on a group of persons simply because of a societal dislike for that social class. The deal is to know what kinds of discrimination are permitted and what kinds are not.

Slavery abolitionists and women's rights, and African American civil rights movements set a precedent in American political history. Three civil rights amendments to the United States Constitution, the Fifteenth, Nineteenth, and Twenty-Sixth— prevent both the states and the federal government from abridging citizens' right to vote based on race, sex, and age. Their tactics to engage people around spreading their ideas and their tricks to influence public opinion and the policymaking process still serve as inspiration these days. The rights gained have significantly improved the quality of life for many in America, especially for minorities. Boycotting and desegregation practices are still prevalent among human rights activists.

7.1 Introduction to Civil Rights in America

Civil rights are constitutionally supported, which guarantees that government officials will treat citizens equally and base their decisions on merit rather than race, gender, or other personal characteristics. In the United States of America, it is unlawful for a school or university to discriminate against a student based on its identity and background. In the 1960s and 1970s, many states still had separate schools where only students of a certain race or gender could study and afford a career. Over time, the courts ruled that these policies violated students' civil rights who could not be admitted because of those discriminative rules.

Although the United States Constitution, as written in 1787, did not formally include a *Bill of Rights*, the idea was proposed and discussed. United States Constitution framers decided to dismiss the bill during the final week of the Constitutional Convention. They dismissed it because there were more important issues to address since the union was still weak and national unrest was still likely to happen. Besides, they perceived that they already had appropriately covered rights concerns in the American Constitution's main body.

United States' founding principles are liberty, equality, and justice. Throughout its history as an independent country, not all its subjects have enjoyed equal access to rights and opportunities, nor have they been considered citizens by law. Discrimination can take many forms, from *segregation to forced mass sterilization policies*, based on sex, income, race, ethnicity or country of origin, religion, sexual orientation, or physical or mental abilities. Federally-funded sterilization programs took place in 32 states continuously through the 20th century in America; for around 70 years, California led the country in the number of sterilization procedures performed on men and women. For much of United States history, most of its people have been deprived of civil and fundamental rights, and sometimes of citizenship itself.

The struggle for equality and civil rights for all continues today since many subjects still encounter prejudice, violence, injustice, and negative stereotypes that lead to exclusion, discrimination, and marginalization.

7.2 Constitutional Source

The Equal Protection Clause of the Fourteenth Amendment only applies to the states and provides that "[no state shall] deny any person within its jurisdiction the equal protection of the laws".[79] There is no equivalent counterpart in the United States Constitution applying to the federal government. Therefore, the language of the Fourteenth Amendment is limited to state action.

Nevertheless, the Supreme Court has held that the federal government's grossly unreasonable discrimination violates the *Due Process Clause of the Fifth Amendment*, where the language applies to the federal government. Thus, there are two equal protection guarantees for each state and federal government. While the protections stem from different constitutional sources, the Court applies the same standards in interpreting those protections and determining appropriate discrimination.

When the Court tries to answer what is permitted governmental discrimination, it applies three different standards based on the classification of persons involved: (1) *suspect classifications or fundamental rights*, (2) *quasi-suspect classification*, and (3) any other classification of persons.

7.3 Discrimination based on Suspect Classifications

The Supreme Court has held that specific kinds of government actions that discriminate against individuals are inherently suspect and, therefore, must automatically be subject to the strictest judicial scrutiny. This stipulation means the government must have a valid reason to discriminate and has the burden of proof, or the party must prove that their

---

[79] For more information, see the Constitution of the United States, Amend. XVI, Sec. 1.

actions are constitutional. The Court determined that there are generally four suspect classifications of people: race, religion, national origin, and alienage. However, this is not a complete list, and as the law develops, the current classifications could be modified, and they may later add more classifications.

Suppose a law or governmental action discriminates against persons that belong to a suspect classification. In that case, the Court will review the law under the most rigorous review called strict scrutiny. Strict scrutiny means asking if the law is necessary to achieve a compelling state interest. If strict scrutiny is applied, the law or government action will be struck down unless the government proves and demonstrates to the Court the crucial or necessary reason for the discriminatory action to accomplish a vital or compelling governmental interest or result.

Instances whereby the government classifies or uses an individual's race and national origin when applying the law, have been closely reviewed by the Court over the last century. During World War II, Franklin Roosevelt issued an executive order requiring people of Japanese descent, two-thirds of whom were citizens, to be relocated and placed in internment camps, where they stayed until the order was suspended in 1944. The order was challenged on equal protection grounds and reached the Supreme Court in 1944. In *Korematsu v. United States*, the Supreme Court decided that laws that treat people differently because of race are highly suspicious, making race a suspect classification.[80] In the majority opinion, Former Associate Justice of the Supreme Court of the United States Hugo Black declared "all legal restrictions which curtail the civil rights of a single group are immediately suspect. That is not to say that all such restrictions are unconstitutional; it is to say that courts must subject them to the most rigid scrutiny. Pressing public necessity may sometimes justify the existence of such restrictions; racial antagonism never can".

---

[80] See Kenney, Karen L, and Friedman, Richard D. *Korematsu V. the United States: World War II Japanese-American Internment Camps.* Minneapolis: ABDO Pub, 2013. Print..

Since the government action, the executive order has used individual's race and national origin; the Court had to apply *strict scrutiny* when asking if the action was constitutional. In Korematsu, it was the only clear racial discrimination case upheld despite applying strict scrutiny. The Court found placing the Japanese Americans in the camps was necessary to achieve *national security's compelling interest*. The Court held there was a compelling state purpose in national security. However, this holding was vital because it set a precedent and legal standard of review that legislators have used to evaluate laws that had discriminated against based on race and national origin.

Becoming a suspect class sounds like a good thing since it means that laws that discriminate against one's group get the strictest level of scrutiny. Nevertheless, it has proven to be a double-edged sword for racial groups because it tends to strike down laws that discriminate against one and laws that discriminate in one's favor. The efforts that groups have had to gain higher levels of scrutiny applied to the laws that treat them differently have been grueling. Moreover, even when the outcome is successful and discriminatory laws get annulled, only de jure discrimination formally is ended, while de facto discrimination may still be prevalent.

In United States constitutional law, when a court finds that a law infringes a fundamental right, it will also apply the strict scrutiny standard to hold it until the government can demonstrate that the law or regulation is necessary to achieve a *compelling state interest*. The United States Constitution protects certain fundamental constitutional rights and civil liberties.[81] If rights are denied to everyone, it is a substantive due process problem. If they are denied to some individuals but not to others, it is an equal protection problem. In either case, the standard of strict scrutiny will be applied.

Various privacy rights, including marriage, sexual relations, abortion, and childrearing, are fundamental rights. Thus, regulations affecting

---

[81] Even if lawyers and political scientists use to make a distinction between civil liberties and civil rights, they have interpreted the United States Constitution to protect both.

these rights are reviewed under the strict scrutiny standard and upheld only if necessary to protect a compelling interest.

7.4 Discrimination based on Quasi-Suspect Classification

Laws that discriminate according to gender do not get the same level of scrutiny applied to race and other suspect classifications. *Quasi-suspect classifications* are based on gender and legitimacy (such as legitimate and illegitimate children), and representatives review them with a less rigorous analysis. When analyzing government action based on quasi-suspect classifications, the Court will apply the intermediate standard and strike down the law or government action unless it is substantially related to a significant government interest. As with strict scrutiny, *intermediate scrutiny* also places the burden of proof on the government.

First, when a law creates a gender classification, intermediate scrutiny will apply. As stated in *United States v. Virginia*, "parties who seek to defend gender-based government action must demonstrate an exceedingly persuasive justification for that action." (Ginsburg and Supreme Court Of The United States). *The important governmental interest* used to justify discrimination based on gender must be genuine, meaning it has to be reliable and cannot be overly broad or generalized. When, in *United States v. Virginia*, a state military school's policy of admitting only men was challenged, the state attempted to justify it, claiming that it offers a diversity of *educational approaches*. Also, that females would not be able to meet the male-only military school's physical requirements.

The Supreme Court found these arguments unconvincing. There was no evidence that that the single-sex school was established or maintained with a view of fostering diversity of educational opportunities, and there was some evidence that some women could meet the school's physical requirements. The state's argument of a vital governmental interest was not genuine and had no evidence to prove their claims were valid.

Intermediate scrutiny is not as hard to overcome as strict scrutiny. Therefore, there are more examples of where the Court has upheld classification or discrimination based on gender. A state law that excluded normal pregnancy and childbirth from state disability benefits was upheld that the law did not create a classification based on gender. The program's purpose was to create classifications based on the risk of disability, and normal pregnancies did not create such a risk.[82]

The Court has also reviewed discrimination against men. Laws punishing males but not females for statutory rape were upheld because the Court found the classification to be substantially related to the vital interest of preventing minors' pregnancy.[83] While other laws that preferred males over females to act as an administrator of an estate[84] or only authorize wives to be eligible to receive alimony[85] were struck down because there was no substantial relationship to a significant government interest.

7.5 Discrimination based on Other Groups' Classifications

All other classifications are reviewed under the rational basis standard and will be upheld unless they bear no rational relationship to any conceivable legitimate government interest. Nevertheless, if the government has no interest in discriminating against a group of persons other than a societal fear or dislike of them, the classification will not meet the standard. The understanding is that for any class of persons that is not a suspect or quasi-suspect class defined by the Court, then the rational basis standard will apply.

[82] For more information, see Stewart, Potter, and Supreme Court Of The United States. *U.S. Reports: Geduldig v. Aiello, 417 U.S. 484.* 1973. Periodical. Library of Congress, www.loc.gov/item/usrep417484/.
[83] See Rehnquist, William H, and Supreme Court Of The United States. *U.S. Reports: Michael M. v. Sonoma County Superior Court, 450 U.S. 464. 1980.* Periodical. Retrieved from the Library of Congress, www.loc.gov/item/usrep450464/.
[84] See Supreme Court Of The United States. U.S. Reports: Reed v. Reed, 404 U.S. 71. 1971. Periodical. Retrieved from the Library of Congress, www.loc.gov/item/usrep404071/.
[85] See Brennan, William J., Jr, and Supreme Court Of The United States. *U.S. Reports: Orr v. Orr, 440 U.S. 268. 1978.* Periodical. Library of Congress, www.loc.gov/item/usrep440268/.

The Court has held that several classifications are not suspect. Age is not a suspect class. Thus, the government action based on age will be upheld if there is a conceivable rational basis for the classification. Laws that force police officers to retire at age 50, even though physically fit as a young officer, or judges to retire at age 70 do not violate the *Equal Protection Clause*. Mental disabilities are also not suspect classifications. The Court struck down a zoning ordinance that prohibited a group of mentally disabled persons from sharing a residential home because the only reason to deny them the benefit was their mental condition. The government has no legitimate interest in prohibiting mentally disabled persons from living together.[86]

Utterly because a law or governmental action results in discrimination is not sufficient to trigger strict or intermediate scrutiny or the rational basis test, the government's law or action must be intentional. The intent is shown in three different ways: (1) *facial discrimination*, (2) *discriminatory application*, or (3) *discriminatory motive*. Once the Court has determined that there was an intent to discriminate, the Court will then apply and look at the law through one of the strict standards of review.

Facial discrimination is when a law includes classifications that make evident social distinctions based on race and gender on its "face" or within its terms. In *Strauder v. West Virginia*, the Supreme Court considered a law that provided that only white males can serve as jurors[87]. In such cases, the Court can then apply the appropriate standard of review for racial and gender classifications. Another indicator of facial discrimination is *de jure discrimination*, which is discrimination by laws. De jure segregation, or legalized segregation of Black and White people, was present in almost every aspect of life in the South during the Jim Crow era: from public

---

[86] See White, Byron Raymond, and Supreme Court Of The United States. *U.S. Reports: Cleburne v. Cleburne Living Center, 473 U.S. 432. 1984.* Periodical. Library of Congress, www.loc.gov/item/usrep473432/.

[87] See Strong, William, and Supreme Court Of The United States. U.S. Reports: Strauder v. West Virginia, 100 U.S. 303. 1879. Periodical. Library of Congress, www.loc.gov/item/usrep100303.

transportation to cemeteries, from prisons to health care, from residences to libraries. Under segregation laws that, on their face, created racial classifications, Black and White people were to be separated, purportedly to minimize violence. De jure segregation, or "Jim Crow," lasted from the 1880s to 1964. *Jim Crow laws* were efficient in perpetuating the idea of "white superiority" and "black inferiority."

In contrast, *de facto discrimination* results from life circumstances, habits, customs, or socioeconomic status. De facto segregation is the direct manifestation of de jure segregation. While the Court eventually held laws that segregated races were unconstitutional, it could not change its people's hearts and minds. If people did not want to be in the presence of another ethnicity or race, they could certainly make this a reality. So, de jure segregation was implemented by law, de facto segregation, shared understandings, and personal choice.

Second, *discriminatory application* applies when a law appears neutral and fair on its face but is applied differently to different groups of people and cultures. If the persons challenging the governmental action can prove that the government officials applying the law had a discriminatory purpose, representatives will likely annul the law. In *Yick Wo v. Hopkins*, a law prohibited people from operating a laundry mat in wooden buildings but gave local governmental officials discretion to grant exceptions[88]. At that time in history, the laundry mats in that area were owned almost exclusively by people of Chinese descent. The governmental officials ended up only granting the exceptions to non-Asian laundromat owners. The law had a discriminatory application based on the suspect classification of race and national origin and was annulled.

Sometimes, a law or government action will appear neutral and fair on its face and its application but will have a discriminatory impact on a particular class of persons. Such law will be found to involve a

---

[88] For more information and insights, see Matthews, Stanley, and Supreme Court Of The United States. *U.S. Reports: Yick Wo v. Hopkins, 118 U.S. 356. 1885*. Periodical. Library of Congress, www.loc.gov/item/usrep118356.

prohibited classification (and be subject to the level of scrutiny appropriate to that classification) only if a court finds that the law-making body enacted the law for a discriminatory purpose. It can be challenging to prove that the government had a discriminatory purpose when passing a law. In *McCleskey v. Kemp*, the statistics and historical facts showing that black defendants in capital cases are much more likely to receive the death penalty than white defendants in similar cases. However, the statistical evidence was not enough to prove that the state had a discriminatory motive or purpose when convicting the black defendants. Moreover, the convictions, the governmental action were upheld. It takes more than statistical evidence to prove a discriminatory purpose.

It is important to remember that the Equal Protection and Due Process Clauses only prohibit state or government action. Furthermore, while private actors are not subject to the *Equal Protection Clause*, they may be subject to other laws preventing discrimination. For example, the federal Age Discrimination in *Employment Act* prohibits age discrimination for people who are age 40 or older. Similar laws prohibit workplace discrimination based on disability, race and national origin, genetic information, pregnancy, religion, and sex. These laws were passed by Congress and enforced by the *Equal Employment Opportunity Commission*.

7.6 The Case of Race

It is essential to understand the origins of discrimination to understand the journey and development of civil rights. Why do some people call slavery America's original sin? The narratives that white slave-owners used to justify slavery created an image of an inferior race that required white mastery. These tales established a set of stereotypes of African Americans that continue to haunt the nation. Researchers have evidenced stereotypes' lingering effects in the relatively recent cases and development of law discussed above. While slavery has not been prevalent in the United States for over a century, racial stereotypes are still prevalent today.

As slavery persisted in the country's beginnings, the landmark decision in *Dred Scott v. Sandford*[89], which held African Americans were not
citizens and could not be free, increased tensions between the North and
South and helped incite the anti-slavery movement. The Supreme Court
came up with the principle of separate but equal. This decision created
a two-class system in America. The Civil War did not settle the issue of
slavery in the United States. The American Civil War (1861–1865) was
fought mainly over slavery, and even the conclusion of that event did
not put the issue to rest. Immediately following the war and the passage
of the *Thirteenth Amendment* of the United States Constitution banning
slavery, white southerners tried to seize back the power they had lost,
bypassing state and local laws.

The laws passed after the Civil War limited the rights of African
Americans. The arena of national legislative politics was closed to African Americans after the North turned to its own affairs following the
Civil War Amendments' passage. Black codes were known as state and
local laws that denied freed blacks the right to vote, go to school, and
own property. The era of Jim Crow laws began. To shut down the black
codes, the Northern-dominated Congress passed the Fourteenth and
Fifteenth Amendments that granted citizenship and the right to vote to
African Americans. *Jim Crow laws* were passed by white southerners that
tried to re-create the power relations of slavery by running around the
amendments designed to give blacks citizenship rights. These were forms
of de jure discrimination that created a segregated society.

While the Civil War attempted and failed to remedy the societal
damage of slavery, Congress and the Supreme Court were also slow with
their efforts. Decades after the Civil War, in *Plessy v. Ferguson*[90], the

---

[89] See Taney, Roger Brooke, and Supreme Court Of The United States. *U.S. Reports: Dred Scott v. Sandford, 60 U.S. 19 How. 393. 1856.* Periodical. Retrieved from the Library of Congress, www. loc.gov/item/usrep060393a/.

[90] See Supreme Court Of The United States. *U.S. Reports: Plessy v. Ferguson, 163 U.S. 537. 1895.* Periodical. Retrieved from the Library of Congress, www.loc.gov/item/usrep163537/.

Supreme Court still did not provide equal treatment of all citizens and came up with the principle of separate but equal use of public facilities by different races and put the seal of constitutional approval on segregation. This established a two-class system in America.

In the 1930s, the NAACP began to use a law school-centered strategy to undermine Plessy slowly. The separate but equal view held a standard that separate facilities were legal if they were equal. Of course, this was not equal at all. This circumstance gestured that the courts would not be a profitable arena for blacks to fight in either. In 1910, African Americans who refused to accept the Jim Crow second-class citizenship organized the National Association for the Advancement of Colored People.

The NAACP's calculation was that to most Americans, law schools would be a less threatening area for desegregation than primary education, but one where the justices of the Supreme Court were particularly well suited to find arguments against segregation to be persuasive. In Brown v. Board of Education, the Court finally reversed its prior ruling, holding that segregation itself was unequal and the separate but equal doctrine that had prevailed in the legal community for more than half a century was unconstitutional.[91]

Even after the Brown decision, the right to equality was fought with boycotts to address systematic discrimination. One year after the Brown decision, when Rosa Parks refused to vacate her bus seat for a white man in Montgomery, Alabama and launched the bus system boycott, African Americans realized that their purchasing power could be a considerable political weapon[92]. This circumstance was to be followed by the quick realization that television's new technology could bring their plight out of isolation in the South to the whole country's attention.

---

[91] See Warren, Earl, and Supreme Court Of The United States. *U.S. Reports: Brown v. Board of Education, 347 U.S. 483. 1953.* Periodical. Library of Congress, <www.loc.gov/item/usrep347483/>.

[92] See Krutz, Glen S. *American Government 2e.*, 2019. Internet resource. especially chapter 5, for an in-depth analysis on how boycotts were used to address systematic discrimination in the United States.

The battle for equality was also fought with public opinion. The civil rights movement was fought in the arenas of public opinion and, finally, in Congress. In 1964 and 1965, civil rights legislation, initiated by President John Kennedy and then pushed through Congress by President Lyndon Johnson after Kennedy's assassination, removed most of the legal barriers to integration. Southern Congress members staged a filibuster to prevent a vote on the Senate's legislation, voting against their party's president. Most notably, the Civil Rights Act of 1964 prohibited segregation in public places based on race, religion, or national origin. It also created the Equal Employment Opportunity Commission that enforces laws that prohibit discrimination in the workplace. The civil rights movement was the combination of all these strategies used to alleviate African Americans' plight.

Did the civil rights movement eradicate de facto discrimination as well as de jure? One irony of all the legislative changes was that it ended the de jure discrimination in the South but pointed out the shortcomings of legal change as a method to redress de facto segregation in the North. Segregation in the North arose from long-term economic patterns and demographic changes that left African Americans in the city centers and succeeding waves of newly assimilated white immigrants in the suburbs. De facto discrimination cannot be remedied by fixing laws. It requires an effort to fix the outcomes, which strikes many Americans as fundamentally unfair. Despite the hard-won changes in laws, demeaning racial narratives were still woven into the American story and still determined how African Americans were treated and fared in rules and institutions based on white privilege.

Does the United States still have a race problem? Racial discrimination endures as one of American politics' defining issues, especially as demographic change forces whites to grapple with sharing minority status with other racial groups. Systemic racism is built into the American system to give whites preference and stacks the deck against people of color. The battle for equal rights does not end with African Americans. People of color who have had to fight for equal treatment by the law also include Native Americans, Latinos, and Asians. The assimilation of European immigrants has traditionally been about their ability to fit in; the assimilation of people of color has depended on the willingness of the white population to give up racist narratives to accept them.

The government has a compelling interest in remedying past discrimination against a racial or ethnic minority. Thus, if a court finds that a governmental agency has engaged in racial discrimination, it may exercise affirmative action, a race-conscious remedy to help end the discrimination and ease the effects. A remedy of this type is permissible under the *Equal Protection Clause* because it is narrowly tailored to further the compelling interest to eliminate discrimination. For example, when it has been proven that a public employer engaged in persistent racial discrimination, a court may order relief that establishes a goal for hiring or promoting minority persons to eliminate the effects of the past discrimination.

7.7 The Case of Gender

The women's rights movement began in Seneca Falls in 1848. Sexism, like racism, is pervasive, often unrecognized, and has deep cultural roots. The women's rights movement is commonly dated from the Seneca Falls (NY) Convention of 1848, where the first women's rights convention was held. The widely accepted narrative that kept wealthy white women out of public life was that they were too good and pure for the rough and tumbled corruption of public life. As with the racial equality movement, the women's suffrage movement was also gradual and spanned several decades.

Women fought for equality across all levels of government. On the western frontier, women worked side by side with men to carve a life out of the wilderness. The state-level effort promised more but slower success for women's rights. By 1912, women could vote in states that accounted for 74 electoral votes for the presidency. The *Nineteenth Amendment (1920)* gave women the right to vote. More equal rights would have required the passage of the *Equal Rights Amendment*. It was never ratified by the states but still discussed in current political platforms.

Modern legislation has called for equality for women. The *Lilly Led-better Fair Pay Act of 2009* requires equal pay for equal work. Women often make less money than men for the same work. The glass ceiling is the concept that women are still a minority in places where power is wielded. *Cultural attitudes* toward women are changing (e.g., the #MeToo movement) and will continue to change.

7.8 Sexual Orientation and Gender Identity

Unlike race and gender, the movement for equal protection for LGBTQ (lesbian, gay, bisexual, transgender, and queer or questioning) is still in its beginnings. It has only gained momentum in the last couple of decades. The movement seeks to accomplish what the race and gender movements have only recently achieved- guarantees for federal and state civil rights and protections against discrimination.

The Court addressed the first step in considering LGBTQ rights in *One, Inc. v. Olsen*, which primarily expanded the right of free speech by establishing that material published for a gay audience was not inherently obscene.[93] The movement had had setbacks in 1986 when the Court held that the *14th Amendment's Due Process guarantee* does not prohibit states from criminalizing sex between people of the same sex. The opinion of the Supreme Court pendulum swung again in 2003 and reversed their prior decision and held that the due process clause gave people "the full right to engage in private conduct without government intervention... [and there is] no legitimate state interest which can justify its intrusion into the individual's personal and private life". (Kennedy and Supreme Court of The United States, Lawrence et. al. Texas)

---

[93] See Supreme Court Of The United States. *U.S. Reports: One, Incorporated, v. Olesen, 355 U.S. 371. 1957.* Periodical. Library of Congress, www.loc.gov/item/usrep355371/.

A landmark decision in 2015 held that the fundamental right to marry under the right to privacy is guaranteed to same-sex couples in *Obergefell v. Hodges*. While the law is slowly moving toward providing complete equal protection for the LGBTQ community eventually, real change will likely be incremental. The movement still has a long way to go.

CHAPTER 8

The Legislative Branch

Chapter summary

To successfully prevent the national government, or any group within it, from becoming exceedingly powerful, the United States Constitution divided the government into three branches with different powers and attributions. Congress can pass laws, but its power to do so can be checked by the United States president, who can veto potential legislation so that it ultimately cannot become a law.

Most of Congress's work activities and work take place in *l*egislative committees. The House of Representatives has 20 permanent committees. The Senate has 21, and there are four joint committees with members from both chambers. These congressional committees have purview over specific issues, and they identify potential issues that could be subject to legislative review. Some areas in which these committees jurisdiction include agriculture, foreign affairs, budgets, and finance. House members from states with significant sectoral interests, such as agriculture, will likely seek these specific committees' positions.

To sit in the United States Congress, almost every member has to run for election and beat their opponent. The Seventeenth Amendment outlines how representatives should fill a vacancy caused by death, resignation, or removal from office should.

8.1 Introduction – What is the Legislative Branch?

The *legislative branch* is one of the three branches of the United States government as outlined by the Constitution. The legislative comprises the two chambers of Congress, the House, and the Senate. The legislative government branch produces the laws, declares war, and regulates taxes, among other duties.

One hundred elected representatives, two from each state, compose the *United States Senate.* It is the Senate's upper chamber and has more powers than the House, such as the power to impeach the United States President and confirm Cabinet positions, Supreme Court Justices, and other positions. Since it has more specific powers and has fewer members than the House, politicians have a more sought-after position. Citizens elect *Senators* to six-year terms with elections staggered, so approximately 1/3 of the Senate is up for election every even-numbered year.

The *House of Representatives* is the lower chamber of Congress, and it has 435 elected members. Unlike the Senate, the House is divided proportionally based on the population size of each state. The seven states with the lowest population have only one representative, while the most populous state, California, has 53 representatives in the House. The House also has powers that are unique to it, including impeaching federal officers and electing a United States President in the event of an Electoral College tie. A *Representative* serves a shorter term than a Senator, only two years, and is up for election every even-numbered year.

8.2 How the Constitution Established Congress

The Constitution outlines the role of Congress in Article I. Article I, Section I, states:

> "All legislative Powers herein granted shall be vested in a Congress of the United States, which shall consist of a Senate and House of Representatives."

One of the key design elements from the Founding Fathers was making Congress bicameral. A *bicameral legislature* is a legislative body that has two chambers. When discussing the government's structure under the United States Constitution, the delegates from Virginia called for a bicameral legislature consisting of two Houses. Delegates from small states objected to the Virginia Plan, which ultimately prevailed.

Another proposal, the New Jersey Plan, called instead for a unicameral legislature with one House, in which each state would have one vote. Consequently, smaller states would have the same power in the national legislature as larger states. Notwithstanding, the larger states argued that they should be allotted more legislators to represent their interests because they had a more significant population. (Corwin, 48)

The two chambers of Congress in the United States were created with different characteristics to represent different interests to protect any region or state from getting too much power. Each state has equal representation in the Senate, while in the House, states with a higher population have more seats and thus more voting power. The House of Representatives has developed a more robust and structured leadership than the Senate. Because its members serve two-year terms, they regularly answer their constituency's demands when running for election or reelection. Even House members of the same party in the same state will occasionally disagree on different issues because of their specific districts' particular interests. The House can be highly partisan at times. In contrast, members of the Senate are furthest from the demands and scrutiny of their constituents. Because of their longer six-year terms, they will likely see every House member face their constituents multiple times before they have to seek reelection.

The foundation of Congress and the Constitution's contents resulted from the bitter battle between Federalist and Anti-Federalist factions. The Federalists supported a strong federal government, while the Anti-Federalists wanted more power in the states' hands. In the Constitution's passage, the Federalists ultimately prevailed, but Congress's structure was a source of compromise. While not all Anti-Federalists agreed between the House's proportional representation and the Senate's equal representation, they also created state legislatures to compromise with Anti-Federalists.

Another compromise to Anti-Federalists was who elected members of the Senate. While the voting public elected members of the House, state legislatures initially elected their state's senators. This setting gave the state legislatures more power over federal policy. State legislatures elected senators until the Seventeenth Amendment's ratification in 1913, which changed senators' election to a popular vote by voters in the state.

The Senate and the House were made with two different structures so that they would represent different constituencies. Each member of government has a *constituency*, the individuals and groups whose interests the elected official represents. Senators represent their whole state when they go to Congress, and until 1913 they were closely tied to political interests in their state's legislature. Each House member represents a district in their state. For example, California has 53 distinct districts. Under this original design, representatives were supposed to represent the people and their opinions, while senators were representatives of their state and legislature.

The two chambers of Congress also have different qualification requirements and restrictions. A senator has to be at least 30 years old, a United States citizen for at least nine years, and be a resident of the state they are running to represent. A representative only has to be 25 years old, be a United States citizen for seven years, and live in the state they politically represent.

8.3 How Congress Does Its Job

To adequately perform the duties given to Congress by the Constitution, the legislative body's structure has various leadership roles. Throughout United States history, the division of power for congressional leadership positions has evolved. Partisanship, narrow margins between the two parties, and the rise in leadership positions' power have marked and shaped modern congressional politics. The Speaker of the House and the Senate majority leader, the majority party's congressional leaders, have all-powerful tools at their disposal to conveniently punish party members who defect on a particular vote.

Most of Congress's work activities and work take place in *legislative committees*. The House of Representatives has 20 permanent committees. The Senate has 21, and there are four joint committees with members from both chambers. These congressional committees have purview over specific issues, and they identify potential issues that could be subject to legislative review. Some areas in which these committees jurisdictions include agriculture, foreign affairs, budgets, and finance.

Initially, Senate committee membership was determined either by a vote by the full Senate or appointments by the committee's presiding officer. In 1846, the Senate changed its rules on committee appointments in order to streamline the process. Today, each party's leadership determines Senate committee membership and submissions to the floor for approval. Similarly, in the House, Democratic and Republican leadership determine which representatives to submit for committee membership approval. This situation gives each party's leadership significant power to keep incoming and incumbent Congress members in line with the respective party's vision.

In Congress, four main types of committees perform different roles and specialize in specific public policy areas. *Standing committees* are permanent as laid out in the House and Senate rules that have specific legislative jurisdiction. In this type of committee, members review and recommend legislative measures and monitor government agencies relevant to their jurisdiction. The Senate has 16 standing committees with 67 subcommittees, and the House has 20 standing committees with 97 subcommittees.

Select or special committees are established for a limited time, often to conduct investigations or research. If an emerging issue does not fall under a standing committee's purview or crosses multiple committees' jurisdiction, a select committee will be set up. While they put these committees in place for a limited time, they can renew them by their respective chamber, and sometimes they become permanent standing committees.

Conference committees are used to reconcile bills passed in both the House and the Senate. The conference committees are appointed on an ad hoc basis when a bill passes the House and Senate in various forms. Congress members sometimes skip these committees in the interest of expediency, in which one of the chambers relents to the other.

Lastly, *joint committees* are composed of members of both the House and the Senate. Joint committees are permanent and mainly perform housekeeping duties or conduct studies rather than doing legislative work. Leadership on these committees alternates between the Senate and the House.

The most influential role in the Senate is the *Speaker of the House*. This position was established in Article 1 Section II of the Constitution, but the office's power has grown significantly in the modern era. The Speaker is the House's presiding officer, the lower chamber of Congress's administrative head, and the majority party's head in the House. The Constitution does not call for the Speaker to have a partisan role, but the role has developed significantly over the years. The Speaker of the House is also third in line for the presidency.

The leader of the majority party in the Senate is known as the *Senate Majority Leader*. Unlike the Speaker of the House, the United States Constitution does not set this position. They are the majority party's head in the Senate and derive their power from their party and various Senate precedents. While the Senate Majority Leader does not enjoy as much formal power as the House's Speaker, they serve as the chief spokesperson for their party in the Senate. The leader of the party with fewer members in the Senate is known as the Senate Minority Leader. The Constitution established the Vice President as President of the United States Senate.

8.4 Congress's Role in the System of Checks and Balances

The Founding Fathers established the federal government as a system of checks and balances so no single branch of government, person, or political interest would become too powerful. The framers of the Constitution created such a system to satisfy the concerns of those who feared an overly strong central government. In this vein, Congress plays a crucial role and has some power over the executive and judicial branch, and vice versa.

Congress has three key ways to check the executive branch, and they give the legislative branch power to balance the President's power. The first and most important is *congressional oversight*. This provision refers to Congress's powers to oversee the executive branch and numerous federal agencies. Congress can review and keep an eye on various federal programs, administrative activities, and policies. The power to create an investigative committee, hold legislative hearings, and set budgets also fall under this category. The Constitution does not explicitly state that Congress has these powers; instead, these powers have been built up over time under the principle of implied powers.

One of the most visible powers of Congress in the modern presidency has been the power of impeachment. Congress has the sole power to impeach a government official and remove them from office. The House has the power to impeach government officials. The Senate can take up the House's impeachment, hold a trial, and vote in the Senate to convict and remove the impeached official from office. The Constitution explicitly gives Congress the power to impeach federal officials, and it also gives the legislative branch the power to bar impeached and convicted officials from running for office.

The House has passed articles of impeachment 21 times, three times against a sitting president. Presidents Andrew Johnson, Bill Clinton, and Donald Trump have all been impeached by the House, and the Senate later acquitted all. President Richard Nixon resigned in 1974 rather than face certain impeachment and a likely conviction in the Senate after the Watergate scandal. President Donald Trump is the only federal official to be impeached twice, and he was acquitted both times.

The final important check Congress has on the executive branch is advice and consent, the Senate's role of confirming presidential appointments, including Supreme Court appointments, Cabinet officials, and ambassadors. The Constitution only grants this power to the Senate and not the House, and it is outlined in Article II Section 2 Clause 2. Initially, the Founding Fathers disagreed about the Senate's role in advising the President on nominations. In modern American politics, this power mostly plays out in high-profile congressional hearings with a majority of senators needed to approve appointments. A two-thirds majority of the Senate is also required to approve international treaties signed by the President.

Not only does Congress check and balance the power of the executive branch, but they also have powers to do the same with the judicial branch. Some of these powers are also within the above powers to check the executive, such as approving or denying judicial appointments and impeach and remove federal judges from office.

One of the leading powers that Congress has to check the judicial branch's power is to amend the Constitution. As the highest court in the land, the Supreme Court takes cases and gives rulings based on the justice's interpretation of the legislation or executive order constitutionality. As the federal courts use the Constitution as the basis for their legal rulings, the ability to amend the Constitution through the legislative process is one of Congress's most important powers.

Congress also has significant organizational power over the judicial branch. The United States Constitution grants Congress the power to determine how many Supreme Court Justices sit on the court and establish inferior courts. The Constitution only required the Supreme Court, but Congress has established a vast and powerful judicial branch with many inferior federal courts. Congress established the district courts system in the Judiciary Act of 1789. Today, there are 94 district courts in the country. Congress also established the 13 courts of appeals.

Furthermore, Congress can also pass laws that circumvent the courts' rulings. While one has traditionally assumed that the Supreme Court has the final say on applying the law regarding new legislation, congressional overrides have become more common in the modern era. William

Eskridge Jr. and Matthew Christiansen found that congressional overrides grew dramatically between 1967 and 1990. While they have decreased after the Clinton impeachment, they remain a relevant tool for Congress to override the judicial branch.[94] Former Supreme Court Justice Ruth Bader Ginsburg asked Congress to override the Supreme Court's ruling in 2013 and said, "Congress has, in the recent past, intervened to correct this Court's wayward interpretations of Title VII."[95]

While Congress has significant power to check the executive and judicial branches, these two branches also have been granted the ability to check and balance the legislative branch. The President's most important check on Congress is the power to veto legislation, thus directing the legislative agenda. However, this power is not ultimate, and Congress can reject a presidential veto by a two-thirds vote. The judicial branch primarily checks Congress's power through judicial review. One of the Supreme Court's primary roles is to review the legality of legislation passed by Congress.

8.5 How Congress Makes the Law

How does Congress go about performing its most important duty, making laws through passing legislation? Both the Senate and House are constrained by the Constitution and norms that have been built up over time. Political interests may influence Congress members, who also have different commitments to their state or district's particular interests.

---

[94] Eskridge and Christiansen state that, before 1975, the United States Congress regularly over-rode Supreme Court decisions interpreting federal statutes, but this mostly was an occasional phenomenon. The big turning point in United States history of statutory overrides was the 94th Congress (1975-1976), where the post-Watergate representatives overrode twenty Supreme Court decisions. Amid political polarization, the 1990s was the golden age of overrides. Eskridge Jr., William N., and Matthew R. Christiansen. "Congressional Overrides of Supreme Court Statutory Interpretation Decisions, 1967-2011." *Texas Law Review*, vol. 92, 2014, doi:https://digitalcommons.law.yale.edu/cgi/viewcontent.cgi?article=5895&context=fss_papers.

[95] For more information, *see* Supreme Court. Vance v. Ball State University. 24 June 2013.

Specifically, in the House, where representatives face reelection every two years, Congress members are constrained by electability concerns. With all this said, Congress is the place all new federal legislation has to go through, and it performs an essential role in American democracy.

Congress members are often drafting and working on bills for years before they reach the floor of Congress, and many bills go through a long and arduous process before they become the law of the land. Bills do not necessarily originate from Congress members, as political interest groups, think tanks, policy groups, and more pitch ideas to congresspeople regularly. Whether a member of Congress presents himself with a bill or ideates and finetunes the whole piece of legislation, the next step for a bill is to be introduced in either Congress's chamber.

The bill's *sponsor* is the representative or Senator who first brings the bill to Congress. In addition to the bill's primary sponsor, other senators and representatives who sign on supporting the legislation in this early phase are cosponsors.

Next, the bill is sent to a relevant committee or multiple committees if the bill spans multiple jurisdictions. The committee then assigns the bill to a subcommittee, where representatives kill most legislation. Here the senators or representatives on the committee discuss and hold hearings on the bill and either decide to kill the bill through inaction or make amendments to the bill and send it to the floor for a chamber-wide vote.

If the bill makes it to a vote in the House or Senate for a debate and vote, a simple majority supporting it will send it to the other chamber for approval. The two chambers have some minor differences in how a bill comes out of committee and debating on the floor. In the House, the House Committee on Rules decides for approval before representatives can debate it on the House floor. A bill in the Senate will be put to open debate, but it can be subject to a *filibuster*.

Unlike in the House, which got rid of the filibuster in 1842, the Senate filibuster allows a senator as much as they want to slow down a bill's passage and take floor time away from it. The practice is a Senate rule and not in the Constitution, and it has become increasingly used in the modern era. The longest filibuster by a single senator was Strom Thurmond's unsuccessful 24 hour and 18-minute attempt to stop the 1957 Civil Rights Act. Thurmond also participated in a 60-day filibuster by multiple senators attempting to stop the 1964 Civil Rights Act. The only way to stop a filibuster is by *cloture*, a vote which requires 60 senators.

Once sent to the other chamber, it faces a similar cycle where relevant committees hold hearings on the bill and make potential amendments before approving it or killing the bill. A bill can pass one chamber of Congress but be voted down or killed through inaction, and both chambers have to agree on the final version of the bill. Once both the House and the Senate approve a bill, they send it to the President for signature and approval. A president can either sign the bill, approve it, make it law, or veto it. United States presidents have historically used the line-item veto and signed statements to influence the laws they will sign. While a presidential veto will often kill the legislation, Congress can override a veto if two-thirds of each chamber votes to override the President.

While this is the standard procedure for a bill to become a law, there are multiple ways that congressional leadership or a congressperson can bypass committee hearings to fast-track legislation through various congressional rules not outlined in the Constitution. If a Congress member asks for unanimous consent to put a bill on the agenda and nobody votes against it, a bill can bypass committees. The Senate Majority Leader can also use Senate Rule XIV to bypass committee hearings.[96]

There are also ways for the Senate to bypass the traditional rules around the filibuster by using *reconciliation*. While bills in the Senate

---

[96] On pieces of noncontroversial legislation, Senate leaders and representatives might use one of two informal processes called clearance and hotlining to determine the feasibility of expeditious or immediate consideration of a measure. The process of passing noncontroversial measures may include bypassing a Senate committee or truncating committee action, even though a committee might well have played a key role in the development of the measure sought to be passed or in the measure's clearance. For more information, *see* Koempel, Michael L. "Bypassing Senate Committees: Rule XIV and Unanimous Consent." *Congressional Research Service*, fas.org/sgp/crs/misc/RS22299.pdf.

require a 60-vote supermajority to avoid a filibuster, the Senate can use reconciliation to pass legislation by a simple majority on bills related to spending, revenue, and the federal debt limit. The Senate can do this three times a calendar year, one per subject.

Another modern development in Congress is *omnibus legislation*; unrelated legislation packaged together for a single vote. Due to their large size and scope of multiple subjects, many congresspeople do not have enough time to read and understand the bill. In modern politics, this creates what is known as "pork," unrelated and sometimes controversial spending that gets attached to bills that will quickly pass. For example, many criticized elements within the various stimulus package deals during the coronavirus pandemic as senators filled omnibus bills with unrelated spending.

8.6 How Congress is Challenged and How Congresspeople Represent Voters

Modern Congress is shaped and constrained by the Constitution, the precedence set over hundreds of years, and present-day political realities.

First, in that list, the Constitution contains the foundation for Congress, both its powers and limitations. The founding fathers shaped the legislative branch's structure after the Constitution's predecessor, the Articles of Confederation, left the then unicameral legislature with some shortcomings. As it lacked power and was challenging to have all the relevant members meet with an impending war with Britain looming, the Founding Fathers saw it necessary to change Congress while submitting it to a system of checks and balances.

While the Constitution set the Congress foundations, the political body has gone through many changes since its inception. As the country has expanded, so has Congress, making the balance of power between big and small states all the more delicate to balance. The country's demographics have changed immensely since the Constitution called for proportional representation in the House of Representatives; one should before calculate by counting each slave as three-fifths of a person for population counts.

This situation leads to the modern political constraints that Congress has. The body is supposed to represent everyone in the country. With diverging political interests and growing corporate power, Congress members are beholden to a wide variety of political groups.

As a rule of thumb, Congress has to answer three constituencies: the voters who elected them, the nation, and their party. In Congress, the people who elect congresspeople all reside in the same state. These politicians are supposed to focus on the *representation* of this group mainly. This political representation means a congressperson has to look out for the constituents' interests in their state or district. Each state is divided into *congressional districts* by their state legislatures. Each member of the House of Representatives represents one of these congressional districts.

In modern politics, congresspeople attempt to represent their constituents in several ways. The first form is *policy representation*, the passing policy that will benefit the people's interests in their constituency. A particular policy proposal may be prevalent in a congressperson's constituency, and voting for its passage is a form of political representation. Secondly, members of Congress often represent their district or constituency by *allocative representation*. These conditions work by a congressperson securing funds for allocating to their district or state that will materially benefit their voters. In section 11.5, "pork" is mentioned, and this is one of the most prominent forms of allocative representation. This obligation also works through *earmarks*, providing taxpayer dollars to projects related to a specific district. Congresspeople also represent their constituents by doing *casework* and solving problems faced by people living in their district and through *symbolic representation*, representing the district and its people at public events.

Congress also passes legislation that impacts the nation as a whole. By the process of *national lawmaking*, Congress passes legislation meant to benefit the entire country. However, it is often perceived as real contractions between the national interest and a congressperson's district or state's interests. Nationally popular legislation can be hamstrung by individual congress people's decision to vote against the popular will in favor of constituents in their district. The tension between national and local interests is inherent in Congress's structure. In case a congressperson does not represent their constituents' interests, they enjoy an *incumbency advantage*. The sitting congressperson is more likely to be elected under these conditions.

Senators and representatives are also beholden to their political parties. Many United States Founding Fathers opposed political parties at the outset of the nation, and President George Washington did not belong to a party. The Constitution does not mention political parties at all. In the Federalist Papers, Founding Fathers James Madison and Alexander Hamilton wrote about the dangers they perceived in political parties. Nevertheless, the pipedream of non-partisan politics quickly dissipated, and parties formed on Federalist and Anti-Federalist lines. While the American political party system has been through multiple iterations, a two-party system has reigned after Washington's presidency.

While the Founding Fathers were concerned about political parties, Congress was established without considering the implications of a two-party partisan system. Throughout the history of Congress and the United States, there have been ebbs and flows in *partisanship*. If a politician is notably partisan, they will fall in line with the direction of his party. If political parties differ on significant, key issues, *political polarization* leads to high levels of partisanship. They perceived that the public's increasing polarization levels were also prevalent within the political parties and Congress. In *hyper-partisanship times*, party members stick strictly to their party line, leading to a *gridlock* in the legislative branch. If there is a divided legislative branch, where each party controls one chamber, and parties have high partisanship and polarization levels, legislators can pass very scarce meaningful legislation through Congress.

The Pew Research Center found in 2014 that Democrat and Republican voters had become significantly more polarized in previous decades.

Beginning in the 1980s and escalating since then, the Democratic and Republican parties began to polarize in Congress. The moderate members in each party started diminished, while more ideologically motivated candidates began to win election to the House and later the Senate. Consequently, the Democrats in Congress generally turned more liberal, and the Republicans became more conservative than before. The moderates from each party, who had earlier been able to work together, were politically edged out. It became more likely that the party opposite the President in Congress might be more willing to question his initiatives, whereas, in the past, it was uncommon for the opposition party to publicly stand against the United States president in foreign policy affairs.

If the legislative branch is divided or the President is from a different party than both chambers, Congress often has to rely more on *bipartisanship* to pass legislation. The two parties often work together to craft legislation and compromise on issues. However, bipartisanship does not solve all the tension and constraints within Congress. Local versus national interests still would play a significant role. All in all, the different levels of representation and how Congress is organized play crucial constraints on Congress's ability to pass sweeping legislation.

8.7 Elections

To sit in Congress, almost every member has to run for election and beat his opponent. The Seventeenth Amendment outlines how representatives should fill a vacancy caused by death, resignation, or removal from office should. In the House, a special election always has to be held when a vacancy occurs. However, the Constitution leaves vacancies in the Senate to state legislatures, so some states' governors are required to appoint someone to fill a Senate vacancy rather than hold a special election.

Other than the difference when a vacancy occurs, Senate and House elections also have other distinctions. Senate elections are more straightforward as every state receives two senators, and these borders do not change. Every six years, a senate seat is up for election, so a sitting senator or a challenger has plenty of time to prepare for an election. In the House, they regularly redraw districts to reflect demographic changes as each district has to have about the same number of residents living in the area. Representatives are also up for reelection every two years, so they often have to campaign and raise money more regularly.

One of the most critical determinants of House elections is how districts are drawn and redrawn. The districts are drawn based on preset rules and political lines. Districts are drawn based on United States Census results held every ten years, mandated by Article I, Section 2, of the United States Constitution. The Constitution sets out that Congress members will use this data every ten years to finalize *congressional apportionment*, dividing up to the now 435 seats in the House.

The number of representatives may fluctuate based on state population. For the 2016 and 2020 presidential elections, there were 538 electors in the Electoral College, and a majority of 270 electoral votes were needed to win the presidency. Once the President of the Senate has read the electoral votes during a special joint session of Congress in January, the presidential candidate who received the majority of electoral votes is officially named President of the United States.

While the Census might seem apolitical, it often becomes a politicized and controversial topic. If someone does not return their census form, he will not be counted. Republicans have long attempted to exclude undocumented immigrants from the Census, and President Donald Trump pushed hard to include a citizenship question on the 2020 Census. The Democratic Party has pushed statistical estimation to represent better who lives in each district, including undocumented immigrants, which would theoretically benefit the Democrats. If a state increases its population relative to other states, it will increase its share of seats in the House and political power.

There are other manners in which the two parties attempt to tip the congressional district system in their favor. *Redistricting* is one of the most politicized ways that the House's make-up is determined, which is the process of redrawing congressional district lines based on the Census results so that all districts remain about equal in population. Every ten years, the state legislature has the final say on how they will redraw districts, and in the end, the majority party in the state legislature has the most significant say. This provision makes state legislatures quite influential in determining the look of Congress. These districts are subject to *gerrymandering*, a highly politicized process that redistricts the congressional lines to benefit one party over another. This situation leads to bizarre congressional districts drawn to include voting populations that the majority party in the state legislature believes will benefit their party. The name gerrymandering originates from Massachusetts Governor Elbridge Gerry, who redrew a district in 1812 to resemble a salamander.

Historically, *gerrymandering* has been used in the United States to change districts' racial composition to marginalize racial minorities. This process of racial gerrymandering was made illegal in the Voting Rights Act of 1965. However, the Supreme Court had to intervene in several cases in the 1990s to overturn *redistricting* and drawing on racial lines. Now districts are often redrawn to benefit one party, known as partisan gerrymandering. Some have argued that this is an extension of racial gerrymandering and still marginalizes racial minorities and other groups. The Supreme Court has ruled that this type of gerrymandering is a political question with a 5-4 ruling on a conservative-liberal line.

8.8 Does Congress Look Like and Represent America?

While anyone over a certain age and a United States citizen can run for Congress, there are high barriers to running and winning a successful campaign. In 2016, the average winning Senate campaign spent $10.4 million, and the average winning House campaign spent $1.3 million.[97] While this money often does not come from the candidate's wealth, it

---

[97] For more information on current spending by campaigns in the United States, *see* Kim, Soo Rin. "The Price of Winning Just Got Higher, Especially in the Senate." *OpenSecrets*, 9 Nov. 2016, www.opensecrets.org/news/2016/11/the-price-of-winning-just-got-higher-especially-in-the-senate/.

often means a politician has to appeal to monied interests, including either the Republican or Democratic Party, to have political success. Although about 40% of Americans identify as political independents[98], there is very little room for citizens who do not want to run in either party to succeed at the national level.

Outside of money spent on a political campaign, other factors determine who runs and wins Congress seats. As mentioned in section 11.6, incumbents have typically enjoyed an advantage electorally. Thus *open seats* without an incumbent are much more desirable. Congress elections also often are impacted by presidential elections to be held in the same year. Suppose a Republican wins the presidency by a large margin. In that case, Republicans running for the Senate and House may enjoy the *coattail effect*, which boosts their chances of winning thanks to a solid presidential campaign from the candidate in their party. After two years in office, the President's party quite frequently will be subject to a *midterm loss* and see their seats in Congress diminished.

And how about the representation of the American electorate? Does Congress look like the voters who elect them? Throughout history, Congress and the American government have had shallow *descriptive representation* levels, how much the legislature looks like the population. While this representation has increased since the times in which only white land-owning males in government, Congress does not have a high descriptive representation level. The 117th Congress is the most racially and ethnically diverse in history, but it is still 77% white[99], which is a

---

[98] Significantly more U.S. adults continued to identify as political independents (42%) in 2018 than as either Democrats (30%) or Republicans (26%). *See* Jones, Jeffrey M. "Americans Continue to Embrace Political Independence." *Gallup*, 7 Jan. 2019, news.gallup.com/poll/245801/americans-continue-embrace-political-independence.aspx.

[99] Among today's United States senators and representatives, the overwhelming majority of racial and ethnic minority members are Democrats (83%), while 17% are Republicans. See Schaeffer, Katherine. "Racial, Ethnic Diversity Increases Yet Again with the 117th Congress." Pew Research Center, 28 Jan. 2021, www.pewresearch.org/fact-tank/2021/01/28/racial-ethnic-diversity-increases-yet-again-with-the-117th-congress/. .

percentage significantly higher than that of the general population (60% white). Furthermore, only a handful of congresspeople are not college graduates, despite only 22.5% of Americans above 25 finishing four years of college.[100] Congress is also significantly wealthier than the general population, and only 3% of congresspeople are immigrants despite the United States having the highest immigrant population in the world at 47 million people.

[100] See the official release of the US Census for more information Bureau, US Census. "U.S. Census Bureau Releases New Educational Attainment Data." The United States Census Bureau, 30 Mar. 2020, www.census.gov/newsroom/press-releases/2020/educational-attainment. html#:~:text=In%202019%2C%20high%20school%20was,from%2029.9%25%20to%20 36.0%25

CHAPTER 9

The Executive Branch

9.1 Introduction to the Executive Branch

What is an executive, anyway? By definition, the **Executive** is one who has the power to carry out plans, strategies or laws. In some countries around the world, the chief executive is a prime minister. The United States does not have a prime minister, and instead the United States chief executive is a **president**. The executive branch is led by the President who is the leader of the entire federal bureaucracy system. The **Federal bureaucracy** is the vast network of departments, agencies, boards, and commissions that constitute the Federal government. In the United States, these agencies include the FBI, CIA, EPA, and so forth. The president is only the head of the federal bureaucracy and not the legislative branch of government, unlike a prime minister who typically has more control over legislation. The executive branch in the United States is tasked with carrying out and enforcing the law as stipulated in the Constitution. In addition to the President, the Vice President and the Cabinet are tasked with aiding the President.

9.2 The Job of the American President

The American President has specific job descriptions and powers and authority that are granted to the office. The key elements of the President's job description are codified in the Constitution and have been granted to the office through Congress and the Courts. The United States Constitution originally limited the power of the Executive Branch, but throughout the history of the American presidency, the power of the President has been significantly expanded. Yet still, the Constitution gives the president less power than many other chief executives around the world. One of the president's most important powers is executive privilege. **Executive privilege** allows the president to keep certain documents that concern the executive branch or national security confidential.

According to the Constitution, the president must meet certain requirements and conditions in order to serve. The Constitution also lists several restrictions upon the office. The President of the United States must be:

- At least 35 years old
- A natural-born citizen of the United States
- A United States resident for at least 14 years
- Chosen by the Electoral College to serve a four-year term
- Succeeded in the event of death or incapacity by the vice president, elected at the same time
- Removed from office only for "high crimes and misdemeanors" by the House and the Senate
- Unable to receive "emoluments" (that is, profit beyond their normal salary) from the country or any of the states

The job of the American president has been significantly modified through the years despite the formal powers granted by the Constitution remaining the same. Several amendments have modified presidential power and each of these amendments to the constitution have addressed changes in society.

The different amendments of the constitution have contributed to defining the roles of the Presidency. The most important amendments to the office of the president have been the Twelfth, Twentieth, Twenty-Second, and Twenty-Fifth Amendments.

When the Twelfth Amendment was passed, it limited and changed how the President and Vice President were elected by the Electoral College. During the first years of our nation, the two candidates who received the most votes in the Electoral College would serve as President and Vice-President. The Twelfth Amendment states that the President and Vice President would be voted in distinct ballots rather than the second-place in the Electoral College presidential election being selected as the Vice President. The change was made to limit the chance of a President and Vice President being elected from different parties. Additionally, under this amendment, the President and Vice President are not allowed to be residents in the same state. In 2000, the Twelfth Amendment became a point of contention in the election of President Bush and Vice President Cheney. Bush was the Governor of Texas and Cheney had lived in Texas for five years while maintaining a residence in Wyoming[101].

The Twentieth Amendment set the official start and end date for a term in office for the President, Vice President, Senate, and House of Representatives. After the amendment, the President and Vice President's term begins and ends on January 20 at noon. Newly elected Senators and Representatives begin their term on January 3, which gives the incoming Congress the power to break a deadlock in the event of a tie in the Electoral College, rather than the outgoing Congress. This section of the amendment served to limit the "lame duck" session, or the time in between presidential terms. It also set out that the vice president takes over if the president dies before taking the oath.

In an effort to limit the power of a popular politician, Congress approved the Twenty-Second Amendment to create term-limits for the President. The amendment was a direct response to President Franklin Delano Roosevelt who served four terms and enjoyed high levels of

[101] Maravilla, Christopher Scott. "That Dog Don't Hunt: The Twelfth Amendment after Jones v. Bush." *Pace Law Review*, vol. 23, no. 1, 2002, pp. 214–270.

popularity leading the country out of the Great Depression and through World War II. The Twenty-Second Amendment implemented a two-term limit for any president. Roosevelt is the only American president to serve more than two terms after President George Washington established a two-term norm as the first President of the country.

The impeachment process to remove the President or Vice President from office is mostly laid out in Articles I and II of the Constitution. But, the Twenty-Fifth Amendment created a mechanism for the president to be removed without impeachment. The vice president and a majority of the cabinet or the Congress can remove a president if they determine the president is unable to perform their job. Near the tail end of President Donald Trump's first term in office, several Democratic Representatives called on Vice President Mike Pence to invoke the Twenty-Fifth Amendment to remove Trump from office[102].The amendment also outlines presidential succession stating "In case of the removal of the President from office or of his death or resignation, the Vice President shall become President."

9.3 The Presidential Job.

The Presidential Succession Act of 1947 delineates additional detail on who does the president's job when he cannot, and it fundamentally changed the Presidential Succession Act of 1886. In the wake of President Roosevelt's death in office in 1945, his successor President Harry Truman sought to change the line of presidential succession. Under this act, the Speaker of the House and the president pro tempore of the Senate were made third and fourth in line for the Presidency, respectively, after the Vice President. The new act changed succession and moved

---

[102] Cicilline, David N. *Cicilline, Lieu Lead Judiciary Committee Dems Urging Pence to Invoke 25th Amendment.* cicilline.house.gov/press-release/cicilline-lieu-lead-judiciary-committee-dems-urging-pence-invoke-25th-amendment.

members of the President's cabinet further down the line of succession, thus not allowing a President to appoint their own line of succession.

In order to govern and lead the country, the president relies on their **cabinet,** an advisory group to the President composed primarily of the heads of the major departments of the federal bureaucracy and the vice president. Each cabinet member carries out elements of the President's agenda. The President's cabinet has 23 members including the vice president, 15 department heads including the Attorney General, Secretaries of State, Treasury, and Defense, and seven other cabinet level members. The Cabinet does not possess any collective executive power, and they have to be submitted to the Senate for approval by a simple majority. While the Cabinet-level positions need to be approved by the Senate, the president can remove Cabinet members at their discretion.

So as no single entity or branch gets too much power, the executive branch exists in a system of checks and balances, and the role of the executive is to make sure that Congress and the Judicial Branch do not usurp more power over other branches of government. In theory, the president has been given just enough legislative and judicial power to hold the other branches in check. While the system is built on checks and balances, the president is the leader of the county and serves as both the head of state and head of government.

In countries with two separate heads of state and government, the **head of state** is a largely ceremonial, apolitical role that rallies the country together. This can be done through the moral or historical influence of the office. The **head of government** is a partisan role, as in the United States, the President serves as the head of the president's political party. Each president utilizes this role differently. A president's talents might suit them better for one or the other of these tasks, for example President George Washington is considered by many to be a great statesman. America, unlike some other countries, has one person, the President, do both jobs.

The Constitution gives the president a limited number of powers, and they are all in Article II, but it grants the president three main executive powers. The president is the chief executive, the commander in chief, and the chief foreign policy maker. As the **Chief executive**, the president is head bureaucrat, making sure the laws are enforced. One of the president's most important powers in this role is **appointment power**. The President has the power to nominate ambassadors to foreign countries, public Ministers, Supreme Court Judges, and various other bureaucrats. As a check on the President's power, some of these nominations have to be approved by the Senate, for example Supreme Court Justices.

The president also serves in the position of commander in chief. In the United States, the **commander in chief** is the civilian head of the armed forces of the United States. The President's exact powers within this role have been hotly contested throughout American history. The President is the commander in chief, but they are not legally allowed to declare war on another country without the approval of Congress. So, the President cannot unilaterally declare war, but if Congress approves a war resolution, the President is considered the head of the operation.

The president is also the **chief foreign policy maker**. As the chief foreign policy maker, the president negotiates treaties with the approval of two-thirds of the Senate. The president also receives ambassadors and represents the United States on the global stage. While Article II of the Constitution grants the president only the limited power to receive foreign ambassadors, this clause is cited to justify the president's powerful and much broader role in foreign affairs.

The president also has a unique power afforded to the office to issue executive agreements. An **executive agreement** is an agreement issued by the president with other countries that enter the countries into binding international obligations. These executive agreements describe how the president will abide by an agreement and can terminate with a new president. An executive agreement is not a treaty, and it is often implemented to circumvent other country's laws regarding the signing of a treaty.

While the president's main responsibilities are related to the office's executive power, the president also has powers of legislative authority.

These legislative powers are part of the checks and balances built into the American system. Every year, the president offers **the State of the Union address**. The Constitution says that the president will regularly inform Congress of the state of the union and recommend the measures he considers useful or necessary. While it is not constitutionally required to be a speech, President Woodrow Wilson began the tradition in 193 of addressing Congress and the American people in an annual address.

One of the President's most well-known powers over legislation is the veto. The **Presidential veto** in the Constitution gives the president the option of refusing to sign a bill that Congress has passed. This is a power given to the executive branch in line with the model of checks and balances. There are two types of veto, a direct veto when the President formally sends back the bill with objections, and a pocket veto where the President simply allows the 10-day review period to elapse, leaving the space for the President's signature blank. While the presidential veto is powerful, it can be overridden by Congress. Two-thirds of the Senate and House are required to overturn a presidential veto. Only 4% of all presidential vetoes have been overturned.

Congress has the legislative power to write and pass laws, but when a president wants to create policy that is not passed as law, the president can issue an executive order. An **executive order** is what presidents can issue to fill in details and enforce the laws passed by Congress. These powers direct the federal bureaucracy to act in a particular way. Executive orders can be overturned by the Judicial branch if they are found to be unconstitutional. Executive orders can also be cancelled or revoked by the President, so when a new President is elected, they often review the executive orders of their predecessor. While executive orders are not mentioned in the Constitution, they have become an integral part of a president's power. Before 1900, executive orders were informal and often not made public, nonetheless nearly every president has made some kind of declaration that can be considered an executive order. Modern presidents have issued many more executive orders than their predecessors. Three presidents, Theodore Roosevelt, Calvin Coolidge, and Franklin

Delano Roosevelt, issued over 1,000 executive orders during their time in office. More recent presidents have often issued several hundred executive orders.

The president has strong powers of judicial appointment. With **appointment power**, the president can appoint judges, with the advice and consent of the Senate, to the entire federal judiciary. Some of the judicial posts that the president can appoint include the solicitor general, Supreme Court justices, courts of appeals judges, and district court judges. **The solicitor general** is the legal officer who argues cases before the Supreme Court when the United States is a party to that case, as it often is. The president also has removal power. While not in the Constitution, the Supreme Court has ruled in several cases that the president has the sole power to remove some federal appointees. The most important case was *Myers v. United States* in 1926 in which the Supreme Court ruled the president has sole removal authority of federal appointees, except for federal judge appointments.[103]

The president also has the power of the pardon. **The pardon power** of the president means the president can pardon those accused or convicted of federal crimes. The Constitution grants the president the power to pardon. In recent years, many presidents have issued pardons near the end of their terms, and these pardons have caused a great deal of controversy.

9.4 How the American Presidency has changed

The job of the president has become more involved as America itself has become larger and more complex. Citizens' expectations of the presidency have grown over time, but the job's formal powers outlined in Article II of the Constitution have not. The Twenty-Second Amendment is the only constitutional change to affect presidential powers, and

---

[103] Supreme Court of the United States. *Myers v. United States*. Oyez, www.oyez.org/cases/1900-1940/272us52.

it limited them by imposing term limits. The founders envisioned a presidency with limited powers; however, many Presidents have expanded the office's informal powers and the formal powers have been broadly interpreted to increase presidential power. And through this process, the presidency has shifted from a traditional presidency to a modern presidency. The **traditional presidency** was a presidency consistent with the founders' intentions of a president with the limited powers set out by the constitution as the groundwork for the powers of the president. There are 19 powers given to the national government from the constitution, and these powers are known as **delegated powers**. The delegated powers are the explicit forms of power given by the constitution to the federal government. In Article I, Section 8, the itemization of powers to the United States Congress includes functions such as commerce, taxation, and declaration of war. In Article II, Section II, the president is delegated powers including those noted previously (Commander in Chief powers, pardon powers, treaty-making powers, etc.).

The presidency also has inherent powers that have built up over time. **Inherent powers** are powers that were not explicitly laid out but rather were implied in their constitutional duty to take care that the laws be faithfully executed. The inherent powers are given to the federal government so that they can operate the federal bureaucracy systems and government according to new laws that have been passed. Examples of inherent powers given to the federal government include the federal government's oversight of food production and the environment in the form of the FDA and the EPA. The government can use their powers to revise warnings and lists to the American citizens regarding food poisoning health matters and environmental impact issues. There are other certain powers not given to the federal government that were thus reserved for the states by the Tenth Amendment.

These powers not explicitly given to the presidency in the constitution are therefore retained for the individual states. These **reserved Powers** are powers listed in the Tenth amendment to the constitution, and it says that the states retained government authority not explicitly granted to the national government. Some of these reserved state powers include public education, public health, commerce within the state, organizing state elections, prisons and police, other issues regarding arrests and incarcerations, highway and road maintenance, and many more. When the constitution allows for powers to be shared between the national and state governments, these powers are known as **concurrent powers.** A concurrent power is known as the power shared by the national government and the state government such as taxation, and the minimum wage.

The executive branch changed significantly and became much more powerful with President Franklin Delano Roosevelt's New Deal. The limited vision of the executive changed with the stock market crash of 1929 and subsequent economic collapse known as the Great Depression. President Roosevelt's New Deal created a variety of jobs programs and turned the government into a much larger employer to help people out of the Great Depression and build the country's infrastructure. The **wide-reaching** social program built infrastructure, public works, and art, created social insurance programs like Social Security to ensure that a safety net existed for the elderly, disabled, and orphaned, and it reformed the financial system to prevent another repeat depression in the future. The New Deal also signaled the birth of the **modern presidency**, and with this the modern presidency grew the role of the president as compared to the traditional presidency.

After the growth of the modern presidency with FDR, the government grew at all levels. Though presidential candidates started promising to do more and more, the formal powers of the office as outlined in the Constitution stayed the same. The presidency had to find ways to expand its power and influence through more informal channels. It did this through the **power to persuade** and convince Congress to support the executive office plans. This could be done by going directly to the people, known as **going public.** The president's increasing capacity to talk to citizens through the media made this method particularly successful. FDR began having "fireside chats" to talk to the American people informally and discuss the state of the nation.

9.5 Presidents, Popularity, and Congress

To be effective, presidents need to have some level of popularity with the public. This is a minimum requirement to be elected; but it may not be sufficient to make a successful presidency. What factors make a president popular? The president often suffers from steadily declining popularity after an initial peak when they take office. Almost all presidents go through a period called the Honeymoon period. This **Honeymoon period** is the first 100 days of a presidency, when the press is likely to be most kind and the majority of the public is giving the new president the benefit of the doubt. Not all presidents do enjoy a honeymoon. Factors like the state of the economy and external events like wars and natural disasters can influence how popular a president is.

A president's popularity is often split between political parties, with the president enjoying the most popularity within their own party. Due to the **polarization** within American politics, the president's approval is often tied in with how popular their political party is at the moment. This limits how the president can cooperate effectively with Congress, and it can help or hinder how real legislative change occurs because these changes require congressional cooperation. If there is a majority in at least one house that is different from the president's party, then the current government is known as a **divided government** and the power of the president can be significantly hindered. In many divided governments, Congress chooses not to work with the president or the president's legislative liaison. The **congressional liaison** is a presidential appointee whose chief job is to coordinate with Congress on behalf of the president to find points of potential agreement and create a legislative agenda.

CHAPTER 10

The Judicial Branch

10.1 Introduction to the Judiciary

The judiciary is an integral part of checks and balances between different branches of government. Alexander Hamilton wrote an essay advocating for the ratification of the United States Constitution called the Federalist Paper No. 78. Here, Hamilton described what the newly created judicial branch would look like and that the judiciary would be the weakest and thus the "least dangerous branch" of government. Through time, the power of the judiciary has changed. The **judiciary** is the branch of government that interprets and applies the law and solves disputes involving citizens and other government actors.

The courts have changed in their capacity to influence both branches of government. The judiciary has become an enormously powerful branch through *the power of the pen*. The Constitution does not explicitly state that the Supreme Court may determine the constitutionality of an act of the other branches of government. However, judicial review of other branches of the federal government was established in *Marbury v. Madison* when the Court claimed this power for itself.[104] The Court held that American courts have the power to strike

---

[104] *Marbury v. Madison*, 5 United States 137 (1803).

down laws, statutes, and some government actions that they find to violate the Constitution of the United States. *Marbury v. Madison* gave the Supreme Court (itself) the ultimate power of deciding what the Constitution means.

10. 2 A Kinds of Laws

The United States is a democracy. In a democracy, laws rule. The **rule of law** is a system in which laws are known in advance, they apply the same way to everyone, and if we feel they have been applied unjustly we can appeal to a higher authority. The laws we notice most limit our behavior and stop us from acting on impulses that are damaging to other people. Laws make collective life possible and even comfortable.

There are different types of laws in the United States judicial system. There are substantive laws, and these laws govern how members of a society are to behave. **Substantive laws** are a body of rules that define what we can or cannot do. When determining what a person cannot do, thereby limiting their freedom, **criminal laws** are a form of substantive law that prohibit behavior that make collective living difficult or impossible. Engaging in a prohibited behavior is considered a crime and subject to a legal punishment. A **crime** is an action that breaks criminal law. When regulating interactions between people or organizations, it is a civil law. **Civil laws** are laws that regulate interactions between individuals or other private parties, such as a corporation. When an action between individuals causes harm against another person it is a **tort,** which is an action that violates a civil law.

Substantive laws are contrasted with procedural law, which is the set of procedures for making, administering, and enforcing substantive law. **Procedural laws** define how the laws are used, applied, and enforced. Court procedures were founded from the United States Constitution's Fifth and Fourteenth Amendment's guarantee of due process which both state no one shall be "deprived of life liberty or property without due process of law"[105]. Due process requires the government to abide by fair procedures before depriving a person of life, liberty or property.

10. 2 B Forms of Law

What form do laws take? Laws originate from different places and different entities have authority to create them. The form of laws and how they are interpreted are important to the judicial system. **Constitutional laws** are established by federal and state constitutions. This body of laws establishes the legal infrastructure of our governments. Constitutions set the framework for the court systems, determine how the three branches of federal government relate to each other and shape the relationship between the federal and state governments. More notably, constitutional law determines how the game of politics is played. Much of constitutional law has grown from federal and state supreme court rulings interpreting their respective constitutions. Constitutional law, and most other court rulings, create **case law or common law** that can be binding precedent. **Precedents** are a series of court rulings of similar issues and facts. These rulings create an authority for courts to apply the same law to future cases that have similar issues or facts.

Unlike case law that was developed by court rulings, **statutory laws** are laws that are made by legislatures. Statutory law is written law passed by a legislative body of local, state or federal government and codified in statute- which means law that is arranged and numbered into a systematic code. **Administrative law** is the body of law that governs the activities of administrative agencies of government. Executive level governmental agency action can include rule making, adjudication, or the enforcement of a specific regulatory agenda. Administrative law is considered a branch of public law. Examples of federal administrative law is

---

[105] United States Const. Amend. X and XIV.

the regulation of civil aviation, planes and pilots to protect public safety through the Federal Aviation Administration.

Finally, **executive orders** are rules that also have the full force and effect of law and are issued by the executive branch, such as the President of the United States or the Governor of a state. They are issued based on authority granted to the President or Governor in their respective constitutions and must be consistent with that authority.

10.3 The American Legal System

Legal systems around the world are different. The American legal systems are heavily influenced by political culture. The United States system in particular can be adversarial and is litigious in nature.

The United States system is adversarial in nature. The **adversarial system** or adversary system is a legal system used in the common law countries where two advocates represent their parties' case or position before an impartial person or group of people, usually a judge or jury, who attempt to determine the truth and pass judgment accordingly. An adversarial system is a system that is primarily concerned that the legal process will be fair, and result in a just judgment. This type of system is different from an inquisitorial system. An **inquisitorial system** is a legal system in which the court, or a part of the court, is actively involved in investigating the facts of the case. This is distinct from an adversarial system, in which the role of the court is primarily that of an impartial referee between the prosecution and the defense. An inquisitorial system is a system in which the truth is the goal and if it requires that the judge leave his or her neutral perch to ask questions and investigate, so be it.

The United States legal system is a **litigious system**. Litigation refers to the process of resolving disputes by filing or answering a complaint through the public court system. A litigious system is a system in which citizens prefer to settle their differences in court.[AM1] As discussed above, if the issue of the case is one of criminal law, the two parties will be the state and the defendant where the state is charging the defendant for violating a criminal law. If the issue of the case is based on civil law, the two parties will be private individuals alleging harm was caused to one or both parties.

10.4 The Criminal Justice System

The criminal justice system focuses on justice. Through the process of **adjudication,** the truth can be discovered, and justice served by providing a formal judgment in a disputed matter. If there has been a mistake in the trial, an **appeal** can be filed, which is a process brought by a petitioner if that party believes there has been a procedural error or that the judge has applied the law incorrectly.

A right given in criminal trials in the United States is a right to a jury trial. The right to a jury trial in criminal cases is found in both Article III[106] and the Sixth Amendment[107] of the Constitution. If you are accused of a serious offence that carries a potential sentence of more than six months' imprisonment, you are guaranteed a trial by a jury of your peers[5][108]. Jury duty is a collective action problem—we all want to share in the outcome, but many of us try to get out of providing the effort that makes that outcome possible.

10.5 Equality and the Criminal Justice System

One of the hallmarks of American political culture is that everyone should be treated the same. But the procedural value that everyone be treated the same is often not the way things actually work in America. The equality for all people, regardless of race, gender and class has not always existed. Even though the Constitution established the **equal protection clause**

---

[106] United States Const. Art. III, § 2 provides "The trial of all Crimes, except in Cases of Impeachment, shall be by Jury".

[107] United States Const. Amend. XI provides "In all criminal prosecutions, the accused shall enjoy the right to a speedy and public trial, by an impartial jury."

[108] *United States v. Nachtigal*, 507 United States 1 (1993).

which provided in part that "[no state shall] deny any person within its jurisdiction the equal protection of the laws,"[109] the judiciary did not originally interpret this to mean equal protection for black Americans. From its beginnings, the United States has had what amounts to separate criminal justice systems for black and white Americans. America has had stronger punishments for those of color. An example of this was the case of Emmett Till. Till, a 14-year-old boy, was caught and lynched in Mississippi in 1955 for allegedly offending a white woman who later admitted she lied. The white men who killed Till were acquitted by a white jury.

The role that justice has served white and African Americans has developed inconsistently since the inception of the nation. There are dual narratives about who are the "good guys." African Americans and whites have developed very different narratives about the role the criminal justice system plays in their lives.

Racial profiling has prevented African Americans from receiving equal access to justice. **Racial profiling** is a violation of civil rights in which police target people because they fit the mental image of what a criminal looks like. Obviously, it is not possible to have a stereotype based on race, gender, or class of a person and profile them as a police target. This difference in application of the law is racism. Racism isn't just what you say, it is also an acceptance of different rules of treatment according to race built into the norms of the system. In the criminal justice system, the issue is *equal treatment*. In the civil justice system, the issue is *equal access*.

10.6 The Constitution, Congress, and the Dual Court System

The founders wanted to avoid having a national court system and chose to root the court system under the foundation of Federalism. Because the question of whether there would be a national court system with

---

[109] United States Const. Amend. XIV, § 1

jurisdiction over the states was such a hot-button issue, the authors of the Constitution tended to gloss over it.

Article I Courts

Only the actions of Article III courts are the subject of this chapter, but it is important to note there are two types of federal courts. Article I courts are created by Congress in order to implement its various legislative powers. For example, the United States Tax Court has jurisdiction over federal income tax subject matters. Judges of such Article I courts do not have a life tenure or protection from salary decreases. Article I courts are sometimes vested with administrative as well as judicial functions, and the congressional power to create such "hybrid" courts has been sustained by the Supreme Court.[110]

Article III Courts

Article III of the United States Constitution states that the "judicial Power of the United States, shall be vested in one supreme Court, and in such inferior Courts as the Congress may from time to time ordain and establish."[111] What this means is that the Constitution provides for one Supreme Court and lower courts established by Congress as necessary. Although Congress has the complete power to set the jurisdictional limits of the federal courts, it is still bound by the standards of judicial power set forth in Article III as to subject matter, parties, and the requirement of "case or controversy" (discussed later). Therefore, Congress cannot require the federal courts to perform nonjudicial functions.

What are lower courts? Most court systems have an entry-level court to which you first bring your case or in which you are first tried before a jury. If you lose this entry level court case, you have a **right to appeal,**

---

[110] *Glidden v. Zdanok*, 370 United States 530 (1962).
[111] United States Const. Art. III, § 1.

which is to ask a higher or appeals court to ensure that everything was handled properly and to review the process.

Federal Judges

The Article III constitutional section also authorizes Congress to appoint Judges of federal courts for life terms. This means these judges can only be removed through a vote of impeachment, so they hold their jobs as long as they behave themselves. In order to be a judge in the federal court system, the Constitution requires judges to be appointed according to certain procedures but sets forth no specific required qualifications to serve as a judge. There are no age, citizenship or other requirements. The Constitution specifies only that the judges shall be appointed by the president, with the advice and consent of the Senate. The judiciary is the only unelected branch of the government.

In order to protect federal judges from political interference or pressures, they receive a salary that cannot be reduced during their lifetime terms. The Constitution gives federal judges this protection so that they can make fair and trustworthy decisions on cases without worrying their decision will be publicly or politically unpopular. Judges can, however, be removed from office only if impeached and convicted by the House of Representatives and the Senate, a process that has resulted in only 15 impeachments and eight convictions in more than 200 years.

Federal Court System

The federal court system is three-tiered. First, the lowest level of the federal judiciary hierarchy consists of 94 federal district courts. Each state has at least one **federal district court** located within its borders while the largest states have four. Federal district courts will hear the case first because district courts have **original jurisdiction**. At this level, the court will consider and rule on all the facts of the case during a trial. Each federal district court has a United States attorney that are government attorneys that represent the United States in criminal and civil cases. United

States attorneys are appointed by the president and approved or affirmed by the Senate for four-year terms.

Next, once a case is decided by the federal district courts, it can be appealed and heard by the federal **Courts of Appeals**. These courts are arranged into 12 circuits. These circuits are large super districts that encompass several of the district court territories. Each circuit has its own Court of Appeals. The 12th circuit covers just Washington, D.C., and hears all appeals involving government agencies. Cases are heard in the circuit that includes the district court where the case was heard originally. The sole function of these courts is to hear appeals from the lower federal district courts if the losing party believes the law was applied incorrectly and to review the legal reasoning behind the decisions reached there. This is referred to as **appellate jurisdiction**. These courts do not hold trials and generally do not consider the facts of the case. The decisions in the courts of appeals are made by a rotating panel of three judges who sit to hear the case. The judges rotate in order to provide a decision-making body that is as unbiased as possible. Having all the judges present (*en banc*) gives a decision more legitimacy and sends a message that the decision was made carefully.

The third and highest tier of the federal court system is the United States Supreme Court and is discussed below.

The judicial ideology is important for the courts because it can sway important legal concepts in the public policy of the United States, such as abortion rights. Judicial ideology varies by the president that nominates a justice. These days an increasingly important qualification for the job of federal judge is the ideological or policy positions of the appointee. The Senate confirmation process has become more rancorous. The nomination process has been more important to conservatives than to liberals.

State Court System

State court systems are different from federal court systems. Each state establishes their own state courts through state law or their constitution.

Therefore, the structures of state court systems vary from state to state. Each state has a tiered system that has a highest court for appeals, which is often, but not always, called a state supreme court. State courts have jurisdiction over state law subject matter and interpret their respective state law and constitutions.

State courts judges are chosen differently than the federal court judges and, again, the procedures are established by state laws. **S**tate judges are chosen through three different methods: Appointment by the governor, election by the state legislature, and election by the state population as a whole. The state election of judges can be controversial. Critics argue that judicial elections can create a conflict of interest because few people are able to cast educated votes in judicial elections. There is a further problem that the political nature of elections and campaigning may influence judges' rulings.

10.7 The Supreme Court

The Supreme Court is the highest court of the land. In the United States Judiciary, the top player is the Supreme Court. The founders wanted the Supreme Court to be above politics. The President is not seen going to the Supreme Court and the Supreme Court Justices are not seen visiting the president in order to keep a perceived bias from occurring. The Supreme Court is still a POLITICAL institution. The very reasons that the founders could not be frank about their plans for the Court in the Constitution shows just how politically volatile the whole institution was. As discussed above, the primary job is to determine if laws are permitted under the United States Constitution and provide judicial review of those laws.

The political nature of the Supreme Court can influence laws, freedoms, and civil rights for all Americans for generations. The Supreme Court is political in three respects: (1) How justices are chosen, (2) How the justices make decisions, and (3) The impact of those decisions on all the rest of us.

It is very difficult to get on the Supreme Court. The president appoints Supreme Court justices, and the Senate approves or affirms the nomination of the president. The president and the Senate consider merit and demographics of the nominee, but mostly the appointing entities are fixated on ideology. Supreme Court justices have always been attorneys, had extensive careers in the legal field and have overwhelmingly been white males. In 1967, Justice Thurgood Marshall became the first African American Supreme Court Justice. And shortly thereafter in 1981, Sandra Day O'Connor became the first woman appointed.

The type of justice appointed to the Supreme Court can either be someone who is a judicial interpretivist or a strict constructionist. A **Judicial interpretivist** is one who believes that the founders could not have anticipated all the changes that make the world today different from theirs and, therefore, that judges should read the Constitution as the founders would write it in light of modern-day experience. A **strict constructionist** is a scholar and judge who believes that the Constitution should be read just as it was written. This is a political hot-button issue now because, until Justice Antonin Scalia's death in 2016, there was a 5-4 majority who were sufficiently committed to interpretivism that they supported the right to privacy and the case that was based on *Griswold*, *Roe v. Wade* (1973).

10.8 Federal Court Jurisdiction

Jurisdiction is the authority of the court to hear the case. The federal courts have jurisdiction over all cases involving a federal question, or **subject matter jurisdiction**, that seeks to answer a question based on federal law or the United States Constitution. Any subject matter involving the federal government or foreign governments would also be within the jurisdiction of federal courts. Federal courts also have **diversity jurisdiction** where the disputes are between two parties that are from different states. Additionally, courts have diversity jurisdiction to resolve disputes between two different state governments. If

Tennessee and Arkansas are disputing rights to Mississippi, the case would be heard in federal court.

Even if a federal court has subject matter or diversity jurisdiction, it still might refuse to hear a case. Whether the court will hear the case (*i.e.,* whether the case is justiciable) depends on whether a **case or controversy** is involved, and whether the other elements of jurisdiction are met. Article III, Section 2 of the United States Constitution also requires federal courts to decide questions that arise out of actual disputes or real cases and controversies.[112] Therefore, federal courts cannot issue advisory opinions in cases involving challenges to governmental legislation or policy whose enforcement is neither actual nor threatened. Although, some state supreme courts do have the judicial power to issue advisory opinions.

A party to a case is generally not entitled to review of a law before it is enforced. Therefore, a federal court will not hear a case that is not **ripe** (case is brought too early). This means the party must have been harmed or there is an immediate threat of harm. A federal court will also not hear a case that has become **moot** (case is brought too late). A "real, live controversy" must exist "at all stages of review", not merely when the complaint is filed.[113]

A person who brings a case to federal court must also have **standing** and show he or she has a concrete stake in the outcome of the controversy. This means the party bringing the action must show an actual injury or harm done and a causal connection between the injury and the conduct complained of (*i.e.,* the injury is traceable to the challenged conduct of the defendant and not another third party). Generally, people do not have standing to challenge the way the government spends tax dollars simply because the person bringing the action is a taxpayer, because their interest is too remote, and the person has not suffered an injury-in-fact.

---

[112] United States Const. Art. III, § 2.

[113] *De Funis v. Odegaard,* 416 United States 312 (1974).

10.9 The politics of making a decision

Getting a case to the Supreme Court may seem very political and, because the decisions of the Supreme Court affect every American and the Court hears a small majority of the applications it receives, it can be difficult to get your case before the Court. In fact, the Court accepts 100-150 of the 7,000 cases that it is asked to review each year.[114] If four of the nine justices agree to hear the case, then the case will be heard. The court can decide to hear a case or not and is generally under no obligation to approve or deny an application to hear the case.

There are a couple ways that the parties can get their cases heard before the Supreme Court. If a party is not satisfied with a lower court decision and wants to get before the Supreme Court, the party can ask the court for review or certiorari. In law, certiorari is a court process to seek judicial review of a decision of a lower court or government agency. Certiorari comes from the name of an English prerogative writ, issued by a superior court to direct that the record of the lower court be sent to the superior court for review. **Writs of certiorari** are pleas from a party who lost in a lower court who believes there is a procedural or legal problem with the previous verdict. Most cases come before the Supreme Court through writs of certiorari.

When a party who is not a party to a lawsuit would like to influence the court to hear a case, the party may write an amicus curiae brief, **Amicus curiae briefs,** also known as "friend of the court" briefs, are submitted by concerned groups. They are someone who is not a party to a case who assists a court by offering information, expertise, or insight that has a bearing on the issues in the case. The decision on whether to consider an amicus brief lies within the discretion of the court. The phrase amicus curiae is legal Latin.

---

[114] https://www.uscourts.gov/about-federal-courts.

When a case goes before the Supreme Court that involves the United States and not two private parties, it is led under the **solicitor general,** who is a lawyer of the federal government and supervises the litigation.

Once the Court decides to hear the case, the parties submit written arguments with a **brief**, which is a summary of the argument and states the reasons the Court should rule in their favor. Next, the lawyers for each party will present **oral arguments** before the Court where the justices are able to ask questions. Often, the justices have already reviewed the briefs before the oral arguments and can express how he or she is leaning when asking questions. The justices then meet in private **conference** to discuss the case and make their decisions.

If a case is to be won by any party, it must receive **majority opinion** of the court, which is the opinion of at least five Supreme Court justices. Usually, one justice is tasked with drafting the majority opinion that represents the views of the other justices. The opinion will state the decision, the reasoning for the decision and sets a precedent for lower courts to follow. Sometimes the Supreme Court will issue **concurring opinions,** which are written by justices who agree with the majority opinion but for different or extra reasons. A **dissenting opinion** is written by justices who disagree with the opinion and want to be on the record even though the dissenting opinion is not considered binding precedent that lower courts are required to follow.

10.10 Important Supreme Court Decisions

Some important Supreme Court decisions over the past 200+ years have provided integral interpretations of the rights guaranteed, although not always explicitly, under the United States Constitution. The judiciary is tasked with interpreting exactly what this means and providing judicial review of laws that may violate these rights. Therefore, whenever the government seeks to regulate these rights or freedoms, the Court will weigh the importance of the right against the interest or policies sought to be served by the governmental regulation.

As discussed above, an important issue decided by the Court was that the Court should be the ultimate decider of what is constitutional in the United States federal government and the states. ***Marbury v. Madison***[115] was a landmark United States Supreme Court case that established the principle of judicial review in the United States, meaning that American courts have the power to strike down laws, statutes, and some government actions that they find to violate the Constitution of the United States.

While the Constitution separates governmental powers among the branches of government, the United States Supreme Court interpreted and specified that the separation of powers doctrine specifically prohibits the legislature from interfering with the courts' final judgments in ***Plaut v. Spendthrift Farm, Inc.***[116] In this case, the legislature, through Congress, passed a law to provide a special motion for reinstating the cases dismissed as time-barred by Supreme Court rulings. The Court held the law providing for the reinstatement of dismissed cases violated the separation of powers doctrine- the legislature can't tell the judiciary what to do.

The Constitution also established the **equal protection clause** which provided in part that "[no state shall] deny any person within its jurisdiction the equal protection of the laws."[117] In 1896, the Supreme Court first dissected the meaning of the equal protection clause in ***Plessy v. Ferguson***.[118] The Court reviewed a Louisiana law . railroads in the state to provide separate cars for white and African American passengers and upheld the constitutionality of the state-mandated racial segregation law for all public facilities as long as the segregated facilities were equal in quality, a doctrine that came to be known as "separate but equal". It took the United States sixty more years to reverse this decision and undo the

---

[115] *Marbury v. Madison*, 5 United States 137 (1803).
[116] *Plaut v. Spendthrift Farm, Inc.*, 514 United States 211 (1995).
[117] United States Const. Amend. XIV, § 1.
[118] *Plessy v. Ferguson*, 163 United States 537 (1896).

damage done with the "separate but equal doctrine". ***Brown v. Board of Education***[119] was a landmark decision of the United States Supreme Court in which the Court ruled that state laws establishing racial segregation in public schools are unconstitutional, even if the segregated schools are otherwise equal in quality.

The Court also declared that the Constitution required equal protection for women when it held that a state law that discriminated against women was unconstitutional in ***Reed v. Reed.***[120]

Certain fundamental rights are protected under the Constitution. Various **privacy rights,** including marriage, sexual relations, abortion and childrearing, are fundamental rights. Modern rights to privacy guaranteed under the Constitution have been clarified by the Supreme Court. In ***Griswold v. Connecticut***, the Supreme Court established a "marital zone of privacy" and the fundamental right of a marital relationship protects couples right to buy and use contraceptives without government restrictions.[121] The Supreme Court has also held in ***Roe v. Wade*** that the right of privacy includes the right of a woman to have an abortion under certain circumstances without undue influence from the state.[122]

Another fundamental right is the **freedom of speech** which provides that "Congress shall make no law …abridging the freedom of speech."[123] The freedom of speech protects the free flow of ideas, a most important function in a democratic society. A regulation or law that tries to forbid speech of specific ideas (**content regulation**) is more likely to violate the free speech doctrine. It is usually unconstitutional for the government to prohibit speech based on its content. In ***Brandenburg v. Ohio***, the Court held that the government could not prohibit political speech, or speech with political content, unless it is linked to immediate lawless

---

[119] *Brown v. Board of Education*, 347 United States 483 (1954).
[120] *Reed v. Reed*, 404 United States 71 (1971).
[121] *Griswold v. Connecticut*, 381 United States 479 (1965).
[122] *Roe v. Wade*, 410 United States 113 (1973).
[123] United States Const. Amend. I.

behavior.[124] However, **conduct regulation**, which is content-neutral and regulates how the speech is conducted, is more likely permitted (*i.e.,* law prohibiting billboards for purposes of traffic safety).

While the Constitution remains largely unchanged and is the most important consideration when deciding a case and applying the facts to the law, the Court has recognized the law needs to be flexible and adapt to changing times. The Court has, and will continue to, overrule outdated precedents.

---

[124] *Brandenburg v. Ohio*, 395 United States 444 (1969).

CHAPTER 11

Public opinion, campaigns, and elections

Chapter Summary

The media can influence the governmental implementation of public policies and the development of public opinion. Policymakers pay attention to both preferences and trends among the public. Preferences are not static and may not remain the same over time. Political involvement relies on how strongly people feel about current political issues. Public opinion polls track and affect election campaigns, the Electoral College and strategic campaign considerations, and the ultimate poll—choosing a president at the ballot box.

Opinions start to develop during childhood, and beliefs subjects acquire early in life are unlikely to change much as they age. The socialization process leaves citizens with attitudes and beliefs that create a personal ideology depending on attitudes and beliefs and prioritizing each belief over the others. To run a successful campaign requires understanding the nature of public opinion and its effects during elections. Campaign managers want to know how citizens will vote and persuade them. Candidates and elected public officials use polls' results to decide their future legislative votes, campaign messages, or propaganda.

11.1 Introduction to public opinion, campaigns, and elections

Why does it matter what the American public thinks about political issues? In a federal constitutional democratic republic such as the United States, the national government, headed by the president, shares powers with the Congress and the judiciary as mandated by the Constitution. The federal government also shares some powers with state and local governments, again as prescribed in the Constitution. The American people elect their governmental representatives to serve their interests and influence the policymaking process.

Political office-seekers often use *public opinion polls* to determine voters' preferences on various issues, so they can tailor their campaign messages to secure the possible votes hopefully ascend to public office. They seek to persuade citizens during the *campaign*.

Public opinion is what the people may think on any given topic, especially on political issues for our purposes. In our representative democracy, there are two ways of determining what people may be thinking; first, by taking a headcount through polling, second, by asking them to vote in elections.

Polling public opinion is very different from "going to the polls" in actual elections. First, in a public opinion poll, for the sake of accuracy, those taking the poll sample respondents to create a group as representative of the voting public as possible during periods leading up to the actual casting of ballots. In elections, however, the voters take the lead and select whom they wish to lead their country, states, and localities.

Second, timing is a crucial element in polling. Researchers can conduct polls whenever an educational institution, marketing company, or media outlet has the time, money, and inclination to conduct them. Elections are different, as they are held on scheduled dates.

Third, polls are not binding on anyone, and one can pay them attention or choose to ignore them while elections are final. Still, public opinion polling and elections are essentially two ways of doing the same thing, finding out what people think at a specific point in time.

11.2 The quality of public opinion

Opinions start to develop during childhood, and beliefs subjects acquire early in life are unlikely to change much as they age.[125] The socialization process leaves citizens with attitudes and beliefs that create a personal ideology depending on attitudes and beliefs and prioritizing each belief over the others. To run a successful campaign requires understanding the nature of public opinion and its effects during elections. Ideally, all citizens would be well informed about government, rules, and relevant political actors. They would also be tolerant of ideas other than their own and willing to compromise to further the collective interest, and happy to participate at various political levels and engage in civic activities. Subjects should receive their news from diverse sources to get in touch with different viewpoints and perspectives.

Most Americans do not always receive their news from high-quality sources, and while they may be theoretically tolerant, they are often less so in practice. Increasingly, some groups have come to view political compromise as a fundamental betrayal of their values. Additionally, United States elections tend to have meager voter turnout rates compared with other democratic countries. All of which leads people to a fundamental question about their government: Whose views should count?

One of the ideals of democracy is *tolerance*, which means that some people who vote in elections may not necessarily be the ones one would prefer. Some voters may even be pursuing a path of *rational ignorance*, that is, choosing not to be informed about politics because the payoff from participating feels too remote or the difference they make seems to be insignificant.

Still, the country may be delivered from an ill-informed populace by specific shortcuts that can lead people toward rationality. Many citizens suffer from a phenomenon known as *online processing*, which is about ending the day with one's head full of opinions picked up on the fly with no clear idea of how one arrived at them. While people often have good

---

[125] *See* Krutz, Glen S. *American Government 2e.*, 2019. Internet resource. Accessed 9 Mar. 2021. Lau, Tim. Brennan Center for Justice, https://www.brennancenter.org/our-work/research-reports/citizens-united-explained, *Citizens United Explained*, accessed 19 March 2021.

reasons for holding their views, sometimes they process them too quickly and with insufficient information. People probably are not as ignorant as they sound. Moreover, they may find that others around can offer them clues as to the nature of things.

The *two-step flow of information* is a psychological process by which *opinion followers* look to opinion leaders for understanding and cues on how to vote[126]. Opinion followers are the vast majority of citizens. In contrast, *opinion leaders* usually prepare themselves through study and research to be well informed and subsequently get involved in civic activities. Journalists often interview them on TV news and talk shows. Some subjects who receive some higher education may become opinion leaders themselves, providing cues and guidance to family members, friends, and members of groups to which one belongs.

Political parties and interest groups may provide subjects with a form of comprehension similar to the two-step flow, except that the opinion leader is not an individual but a group. Still, one should bear in mind that these shortcuts are not foolproof. There is no guarantee that these shortcuts will lead to decision-making that is, in fact, informed and smart.

11.3 How to know what Americans think?

The science of public opinion polling has come a long way. According to The Gallup Organization, a Washington, D.C.-based analytics company founded in 1935, polls can accurately "tell what proportion of a population has a specific viewpoint."[127]

---

[126] See Zaller, especially chapter 9, to better understand two-sided and two-step information flows. Zaller, John. *The Nature and Origins of Mass Opinion*. Cambridge University Press, 2011.
[127] Even if polls tell one what proportion of the population has specific viewpoints and shares certain ideas, their purpose is not to change one's mindset. Social researchers are the ones who explain why people believe as they do and what to do about that. For more information, *see* Nielsen, Eric. What Is Public Opinion Polling and Why Is It Important?, *Gallup World Poll*, http://media.gallup.com/muslimwestfacts/pdf/pollingandhowtouseitr1dreveng.pdf, accessed 15 March 2021.

The modern science of public opinion polling is quite complex. Although statisticians have determined that a random sample of only 1,000 to 2,000 people can be very representative of a state or the country as a whole, modern polling consists of numerous methodologies, techniques, and considerations. For example:

A *random sample* is a representative subset of a larger population in which everyone has an equal chance of being chosen, and no one group is over-represented. *Sample bias*, however, is when one part of the population has been accorded disproportionate weight. One of the most challenging parts of polling these days is persuading people who may be busy or distracted to offer their responses to questions. A *nonresponse bias* may occur in polls if a particular group is less likely to respond than another. To compensate for any sampling bias, polling companies may use a statistical process called *weighting*. Some groups are given more weight to make the results more accurately reflect what the wider public is thinking. Still, in the end, it is an inexact science, and no poll will be perfect.

One way of narrowing the sample is by taking *likely voter polls*, that is, by questioning people who are the most likely to vote in a forthcoming election. In this effort, pollsters may use *likely voter screens*, which are methods that attempt to weed out nonvoters. Furthermore, no matter what techniques pollsters use, polls' accuracy will always be problems, generally called *sampling errors*. Polls may also be skewed by house effects or how a pollster's results favor Democrats or Republicans. Thus, in light of all this, one finds that all polls will vary at least slightly. Sometimes, in an attempt by media outlets to arrive at more accurate results, methods may be used that pull together the results of several polls in what one calls *polling aggregators*.

Polling came into its own when enough Americans owned telephones to make spot digit dialing an effective way to draw a random sample. *Random digit dialing* was how pollsters could randomly sample Americans by calling them on their landlines. Different kinds of national polls measure where Americans stand on particular issues that are released periodically by major media organizations. *Tracking polls* show data movements over periods to detect changes in support for people or issues. They can be particularly helpful to those running for political office, enabling them to see how they are doing than their opponents.

Researchers take *exit polls* as people leave their places of voting immediately after casting their ballots. The raw data are sometimes leaked early, before the polls close, creating false expectations of who might win or even influence the eventual results. *Fake polls* are sometimes released to manipulate results, but they tell nothing about the real world. The upshot is that polls, in general, are notably informative if researchers conduct them scientifically, but any individual poll can suffer from sampling errors.

11.4 How do subjects form their opinions?

What elements may combine to shape one's political views when gathering and processing information? For one, a transfer of political attitudes, narratives, and beliefs from one generation to another, called *political socialization*, probably contributes to one's outlook. It helps create a stable, loyal citizenry who buys into the system's foundational values by bringing people together around shared values. Some of the socialization agents are families, schools, religious institutions, peer groups, and the media. *Patriotism*, or shared loyalty to one's country and its institutions, is also a potent socialization agent.

Still, some agents may socialize citizens to break into separate groups. Socialization works through a set of interests and values that tend to divide people according to ideologies. *Party identification*, or which political party one identifies with, is probably the most significant influence on one's opinions and votes. Party identification is not a randomly assigned feature to subjects. Data can reveal to researchers critical information concerning this vital component of political socialization.

Race and ethnicity play significant roles in determining party affiliations. Over time, the Republican Party has become whiter, and one sees that African Americans are far more likely to be Democrats, at about a ten-to-one ratio. So are Latinos and Asian Americans, both at two-to-one. There is also a clear *gender gap* in that women are more likely to be Democrats than are men, who are more likely to be Republicans. This situation is even more evident in the case of millennials than in previous generations. *Religion* may also play a role in party affiliation. White evangelical Protestants are much more likely to be Republicans, while Roman Catholics split along ethnic lines, and religiously unaffiliated people are predominantly Democrats. *Education* factors into party alliances, with more-educated voters moving in recent years toward the Democrats. The *location* has become another determinant factor nowadays, with Democrats tending to cluster in urban and, increasingly, suburban areas. Republicans, on the other hand, tend to live in outer suburban and rural areas.

The generations into which people of varying ages may fall also seem to influence how they vote. All the trends one has discussed here become increasingly more robust as the voter pool gets younger over time. Democrats are what journalist and data analyst Ron Brownstein[128] calls the *coalition of the ascendant*—that is, of the racial and ethnic groups getting more prominent and more visible. Republicans are becoming smaller and aging out, what Brownstein calls the *coalition of restoration*—a group composed of older, blue-collar, evangelical rural whites who want to "restore" the last century's social order. Brownstein's research suggests that without a change in the current trends, the parties' gulf will only widen when post-millennials begin to come of age in the next few years.

People may identify with a party initially because it takes policy positions that they agree with, but eventually, the party can become a kind of information shorthand for them. As Americans become more polarized, adopting "*Us vs. Them*" attitudes, voters are becoming less likely to leave their party's comfort zone to vote with the other.

---

[128] *See* Brownstein, Ronald and National Journal. "The Clinton Conundrum." *The Atlantic*, 17 April 2015, www.theatlantic.com/politics/archive/2015/04/the-clinton-conundrum/431949.

If partisanship is remarkably important in shaping voters' opinions, do natural and practical concerns even matter? Well, some voters will not consider voting for a candidate who does not share their views on one issue that they consider to be fundamental, regardless of party. One refers to them as *single-issue voters*. A growing segment of voters, perhaps as much as thirty percent, eschew any party affiliations. Researchers call them *independent voters* or swing voters. The upshot is that whether one chooses to act on party cues or other socialization influences may depend on whether a particular candidate can motivate people to vote.

11.5 The ultimate poll is voting in elections

The United States has one of the lowest voter participation rates among industrialized democratic nations. *Voter turnout* is the percentage of eligible voters who cast ballots, and efforts to legally limit who can vote are known as *regulating the electorate*. These efforts to determine who is allowed to vote, which reached a peak in the decades following the United States Civil War, are still alive and well, even resurging in recent years.

The voters who reliably tend to vote are older, whiter, wealthier, and more educated Americans. Younger voters, newer voters, people of color, single moms, and people lower on the socioeconomic scale are less likely to vote, and if they do, they are more likely to vote for the Democrats.

The voters who reliably tend to vote are older, whiter, wealthier, and more educated Americans. Younger voters, newer voters, people of color, single moms, and people lower on the socioeconomic scale are less likely to vote, and if they do, they are more likely to vote for the Democrats. Republicans reportedly want to make voting less open, and Democrats want to make it simpler for everyone. Republicans have expressed their concerns about voter fraud, specifically people who are not legal voters casting votes, so they want to tighten regulations.

The political stakes in regulating the electorate are high. The continuing battles about regulating the electorate are a political struggle over which party will have the advantage. Since about 2010, Republicans have found it easier to regulate folks out of the electorate than to reach out to groups that tend to vote against them.

The political stakes in regulating the electorate are high. The continuing battles about regulating the electorate are a political struggle over which party will have the advantage. Since about 2010, Republicans have found it easier to regulate folks out of the electorate than to reach out to groups that tend to vote against them.

So, if Americans stopped regulating the electorate, would the United States voter turnout rates increase? Studies show that voter turnout rates would probably increase if Americans decided to reduce the legal barriers to voting. Studies also show that voter fraud is not the problem that Republicans claim it is. Still, one would not achieve 100 percent turnout rates in the United States, as some potential voters have many personal reasons for not voting. They do not have time in their busy schedules to inform themselves enough to care about their voting issues. According to their mindset, their votes will not make a difference, and thus, they do not feel engaged or connected with American society. These citizens perceive there are no meaningful offers to choose from, or it may seem to them that all the available choices are corrupt.

Sometimes their parties do not engage in *voter mobilization*; they fail to make an effort to get out the votes of people who would support them. Encouraging party members to go to the polls can also be referred to as *get-out-the-vote (GOTV)* efforts. As one has seen above, this is a burden that tends to weigh more heavily on Democrats.

What difference does it make if people do not vote? People's decisions not to vote or their failure to exercise their rights affect the Democrats more than the Republicans, and not voting can reduce an elected government's legitimacy. An endorsement from the voters to govern is called an *electoral mandate*. The upshot is that voting is of great importance so that policymakers, politicians, and researchers account for everyone's policy preferences, and people can feel invested in their government's actions.

11.6 Presidential elections

The ones that usually attract the most attention are the *general elections* held every four years. On the ballot are the president, every member of the House of Representatives, one-third of the Senate, various state and local offices, and any petition initiatives that may make the ballot in some states.

What are the requirements to run for president? Which are the steps to follow? There are three critical steps in the election process:

The first step usually takes place behind the scenes. The *invisible primary* is when candidates test the waters to see if they can obtain support and promises of big money without launching a viable campaign.

The second step is about *getting the nomination. Party primaries* are held, statewide elections among members of the same party, or in some states, *party caucuses*, which are meetings where party members may debate the merits of the various candidates, and delegates can then decide for whom they wish to stand. The earlier state contests attract many candidates and media attention, so naturally, everyone wants to be among them. However, New Hampshire and Iowa have made it their business to remain first in line. *Frontloading* is a process by which states try to move their primaries or caucuses to earlier dates, which may not be suitable for democracy. Only the most fervent party activists are paying attention to politics that early in the season. During the primary season, the goal is to be the front runner and hold on to that position through the final contest. The *front runner* is the leader of the pack, as seen in the polls.

Candidates attempt to grab and keep the *momentum* by winning debates and maintaining an advantage in the early contests. If, for some reason, one does not perform as well as one has set up the media to expect, one may look like a loser, which can diminish the momentum during the campaign.

The third step is about rallying the party in the *national nominating conventions*, which are party conventions held near the end of summer or early in the autumn before the election, offering a chance to bring the party together behind a political candidacy. Conventions are party mending, strengthening, and rallying events that the media does not have serious interest in covering. The upshot is that most voters will not be paying close attention until the summer ends in the election year.

11.7 The general election and the Electoral College

The general election campaigns open on Labor Day, even though it may feel like they have been going on forever by then. The campaigns keep their eyes on the ultimate prize--more valuable even than the popular vote! When it comes to presidential elections, the final prize is the *Electoral College*, a body of electors from each state who votes for the president. When a citizen votes for a presidential candidate, one is doing it for a delegate (or an elector) to the Electoral College. He will ultimately go on to vote for one's candidate on behalf of the state.

The Electoral College's inner workings may appear mysterious to the average citizen, established in the United States Constitution in 1787 as a compromise between electing a president by a vote in Congress or a popular vote in an election. State distribution indicates electoral votes. Each state has a certain number of electors equal to their total number of Congress members, including two senators. Except for two, Maine and Nebraska, all states cast all their votes to their state's plurality winner. Any state can change its method of how to allocate its votes. The critical point is that different allocation methods may produce different winners and losers.

The Electoral College has a significant impact on candidates' campaign strategies. Some states have much higher elector payoffs than others, and some states are not really in contention. The political coloring book with which candidates concern themselves is red, blue, and purple. While these colors do not have any significance in and of themselves, they are a media convention that has become a tradition. Those states that are not reliably Democratic blue or Republican red, even though they may trend one way or the other in a given election, are called swing states.

These "purple" political entities have become the battlegrounds in which elections are ultimately contested. There are also swing voters who do not reliably vote for either party and must be vigorously courted by aspiring officeholders' campaigns because they often display a resistance toward traditional candidates. Independents become independents because one is repelled by the current political system--by the self-dealing and arrogance of politicians and political parties.

Winning campaigns are usually notable for having competent teams behind them. These days, campaigns are professional organizations. Generally, the campaign with the most money, expertise, and best data-gathering operation will be able to out-strategize and out-perform those that may be less adept. Also increasingly necessary to gain access to the winner's circle is a solid and memorable message. Most swing voters will want to know what a candidate stands for before casting ballots for them. Thus, citizens expect candidates to clearly explain why they are running for office and towards which goals and objectives. They may also search for *wedge issues*, political disputes that they can use as levers to divide an opponent's voting coalition.

Furthermore, because paid advertising is incredibly costly for any campaign, one of the campaign's first goals is to maximize free coverage by staging events and making appearances that the media will cover. Still, for candidates, a good commercial that goes viral and is seen multiple times on cable news and the internet without paying for it is a great thing. *Negative advertising*, or criticizing the opponent, even without mentioning the advertising candidate's name, runs the risk of turning people off and restraining them from coming out to vote. Still, if the issue over which a candidate goes negative connects with the voters, it may prove to be an effective strategy. *Issue advocacy ads* help a candidate by promoting his or her issues or criticizing the opponent's stances.

One absolute certainty is that advertising requires money, and money is a resource to which candidates devote a great deal of their time chasing. Campaign finance law limits how much hard money an individual can donate (currently $2,900 per election).[129] *Hard money* is those funds donated directly to a candidate, *while soft money* is that they give to parties and other groups that can spend it on a candidate's behalf. Wealthy individuals spend *dark money* without having to identify themselves. *Citizens United v. Federal Election Commission* (2010) was a Supreme Court decision that tilted the financial playing field of elections toward corporations, outside groups, and wealthy donors by allowing them to spend without limit and without identifying themselves.[130]

The court's 5-4 majority opinion held that limiting "independent political spending" violated the right to free speech. In doing so, it overturned election spending restrictions that dated back more than a century. The court ruled that there was no threat of corruption if the spending was not coordinated with a candidate's campaign. The upshot of all this is that elections are big business, and all of the citizens are stakeholders in them and in their results, which will significantly affect our lives.

---

[129] The Federal Election Commission clearly states the contribution limits, *see* Contribution limits, https://www.fec.gov/help-candidates-and-committees/candidate-taking-receipts/contribution-limits/, Federal Election Commission, accessed 19 March 2021.

[130] Dark money is usually election-related spending where the source is disclosed or secret. Citizens United contributed to a major jump in this type of spending, which often comes from nonprofits that are not required to reveal their donors. See Tim Lau and Brennan Center for Justice for more details.

CHAPTER 12

Bureaucracy

12.1 What Is Bureaucracy and Why Do We Need It?

Bureaucracy comes from the French *bureaucratie* – from *bureau* (office) and *cratie* (power) – and it originally indicated the group of officials who, divided into various hierarchical levels, carry out the functions of the public administration in the state. In this broad sense, bureaucracy is a hierarchical structure that operates following precise rules. At the same time, bureaucracy has been widely considered as being the most efficient form of organization achieved so far - at least at the level of the ideal model - since it is a functional structure for the management of large quantities of work. Hence, this term does not only define political management, but any set of officials of a body, who in some way conduct the management of this organization (Albrow 1970; 16-30).[131]

Drawing from these features, there have been several definitions of bureaucracy in the literature, of which the most famous is Max Weber's definition of **bureaucracy** as: "an organization where tasks are divided among technical specialists who devote their full working capacity to the organization and whose activities are coordinated by rational rules,

---

[131] Albrow M. (1970), *Bureaucracy*, Macmillan International Higher Education, New York.

hierarchy and written documents".[132] According to Weber, bureaucracy was an improvement compared to previous societal forms of political management and it was necessary to resolve many political issues in current societies. Whereas in ancient democracies, such as the Athenian one, small dimensions of the republic and a conception of political involvement based on liberty as self-government required the whole citizenry to take part in the political management of the community, current societies are too complex and large to grant equal direct political participation to each citizen. For this reason, current political systems have shifted towards representative forms of government, which means that citizens elect ruling elites which are afterwards in charge of the political decisions of the country (Manin 1997; 67-80).[133]

Representative systems yet encompass certain problematic features from a democratic point of view, since elections are simultaneously aristocratic and democratic. On the one hand, elections are aristocratic because they do not produce similarity between rulers and ruled, rather the opposite. Elections tend to create aristocracies, since they select candidates that prove to have the politically relevant qualities and that are deemed superior by the dominant values in the culture. Yet, on the other hand, elections are also democratic: even if there is inequality regarding who can be selected, citizens possess an equal power in deciding who is worth assuming a certain position (Manin 1997; 156-160).

This dual character is reflected by bureaucracy, since this mechanism can be good at some things - making decisions quickly and consistently and maximizing expertise - but at the same time it can also be easily corrupted because of the lack of transparency and democratic accountability. For this reason, bureaucracy has been a central topic of study in political science over the last centuries. That is, political literature has

---

[132] Weber, M. (1978). Bureaucracy. In Economy and society: An outline of interpretive sociology. Trans. and ed. G. Roth and C. Wittich. Berkeley: University of California Press.
[133] Manin B. (1997), *The Principles of Representative Government*, Cambridge University Press, Cambridge.

tried to explain why certain public policy decisions are preferred over others and how relevant officials in the government use these policies to protect or promote their own agency's special interests against other bodies. To understand this debate better, it is first essential to consider how bureaucratic theory has developed over time and how it has been connected to the development of modern society.

12.2 The Framework and History

Bureaucracy is a result of both an economic and political development of our societies. On the one side, the development and enlargement of capitalist industries required economic companies not only to employ more employees, but also more technical and managerial personnel within the industry to deal with the increased managerial requirements of these businesses. On the other side, the expansion of the State into new areas of welfare provision and economic regulation, and the emergence of a mass political party required the expansion of a bureaucratic administration. In this regard, bureaucratization has become a universal feature of modern society and because of its indispensability, any modern organization must rely on some form of bureaucratic management to carry out its tasks. In Weber's words (1968; 223)[134]: "the choice is only between bureaucracy and dilettantism in the field of administration".

Bureaucratization was thus the management response to the development of the territorial state and the capitalist economy, whose administrative needs could not be met by traditional means employed by previous societies. In this regard, the wave of democratization that has occurred in western societies over the last centuries has played a significant part in fostering bureaucracy's importance. Democracy has levelled traditional status differences by requiring a system operating on the basis of impartiality between citizens and by offering opportunities

---

[134] Weber M. (1968), *Economy and Society. An Outline of Interpretative Sociology*, Bedminister Press, New York.

for bureaucratic careers that are linked to education and merit rather than family status only.

However, democracy did not foster bureaucratic development by itself, since this latter has always been intertwined with another process typical of modern societies, namely the process of **rationalization**. This latter can be defined as the historical drive towards a world in which "one can, in principle, master all things by calculation" (Weber 1946 [1919]; 139).[135] As for bureaucracy, rationalization processes can be found in many different spheres of society. In the economy, modern capitalism depends on a calculable process of production structured on division of labor, centralization of production control and other processes that enhance the calculability of the production process. For what concerns the legislative and administrative sphere, precise rules, an autonomous judiciary and a professional bureaucracy enhance the predictability in the sociopolitical environment, thus making it easy to govern a large mass society.

This process of rationalization has become so intertwined with modern society that it has influenced the people's values and identity. It is in this regard that Weber maintained that modern organizations require a "person of vocation", namely a rational personality type connected to the protestant ethic (Weber 1946; 140-141). Hence, according to Weber, the interplay between rationalization and bureaucracy structured modern rational western civilization in three main regards.[136]

First, rational action presupposes *knowledge* of the ideational and material circumstances structuring the action. To act rationally is to act conscious of the consequences of the action and it thus requires a means-ends relationships in order to maximize the outcome of the action with the least expenditure of resources. Weber called this process 'intellectualization', whereby modern knowledge replaces old metaphysics based on superstitions and irrational thoughts. Second, rational processes must be *impersonal and objective*. For example, workers in industrial capitalism

[135] Weber M. (1919), "Science as a Vocation", in Gerth. H.H., and Wright Mills C. (1946), *From Max Weber: Essays in Sociology*, Oxford: Oxford University Press.
[136] Brubaker R. (1992), *The Limits of Rationality*, London: Routledge.

are reduced to sheer numbers and non-economic considerations are not relevant to their judgment. In the same way, rules obey formal codes and apply equally to all the citizenry. Third, *control* is essential, since technological and scientific development have offered societies the chance to impose their mastery not only over nature, but also over human beings' social life. It is in this regard then that a rational and disciplinary ethos has increasingly penetrated into every aspect of social life.

Finally, bureaucracy and rationalization are also connected because the latter is essential in giving bureaucracy a different source of legitimacy than traditional powers. That is, while traditional societies relied on societal custom and habit to legitimize their power, modern societies achieved this legitimation simply by adhering to precisely defined rules, such as following the conduct of office, governing the criteria for appointment and the scope of authority (Albrow 1970; 84.91). In a nutshell, bureaucracy imposed itself as an indispensable system of administration rooted in the requirements of the modern world, since it allowed governments to coordinate action over a large area, to ensure continuity of operation, to acquire a monopoly of expertise and to guarantee an internal social cohesion and morale.

However, the development of bureaucracy did not lead to positive consequences only, since it also paved the way to political debates concerning its efficiency and negative consequences. One of the first debates arose regarding the **patronage system,** namely the political system where the appointment or hiring of a person to a government post is decided on the basis of partisan loyalty. By means of this system, elected officials had the opportunity to use their power to reward the people who helped them win and maintain office. Originally, proponents of patronage sustained that it promoted direct accountability of those who were selected and it also diminished elitism in politics by allowing commoners to occupy important roles.[137]

---

[137] Pollock, J.K. (1937), "The cost of the patronage system.", *The Annals of the American Academy of Political and Social Science*, 189 (1), 29-34.

Political patronage has a long history in the United States, since it was already included in the Article 2 of the constitution. In this article, it is specified that the President has powers of appointment to choose a large number of U.S. officials, such as ambassadors, agency heads, military office and other high-ranking members of government. This power is yet not absolute, since the Senate has confirmation powers to check this selection. Nonetheless, this practice has often been a powerful political tool for the President. For this reason, appointments became so widespread that they formed a '**spoils system**', namely a political organization where the political party which won the elections gives high-ranking civil service jobs to its supporters, both as a reward for working toward victory and a way to make sure that they continue working for the party after the victory.[138]

This process is different from a merit system in which offices are assigned independently of political affiliation and according to impartial procedures meant to award candidates on the basis of some measure of merit. This difference created problems at the end of the 19th century, when 'spoils system' became too widespread, especially at local level, thus giving political leaders the opportunity to dominate local government and politics by building a community of supporters whose main aim was to maintain power from one election to another. Hence, patronage encompasses also several deficiencies that may erode public confidence in this system, since it can favor corruption and it can create a system where those appointed are unlikely to speak freely and to criticize their bosses on whom their job depends.[139]

For this reason, at the end of the 19th century, the Pendleton Act of 1883 shifted the appointment process to a merit-based system, in which recruitment was made by means of competitive exams meant to assess

---

[138] Folke, O., Hirano S., and Snyder Jr J.M. (2011), "Patronage and elections in US states.", *American Political Science Review*, 105 (3), 567-585.
[139] Friedrich C.J. (1937), "The rise and decline of the spoils tradition.", *The Annals of the American Academy of Political and Social Science*, 189 (1), 10-16.

competence rather than partisan affiliation. In this way, **neutral competence** became the primary selection method and rulers used it to deliver the message that in an ideal bureaucratic structure power is hierarchical and rule based. That is, a well-functioning bureaucratic system must appoint individuals according to their expertise and it must promote bureaucrats on the basis of merit, not personal affiliations. In this way, a neutral bureaucratic organization can make decisions better and more quickly than a patronage system and even than a democracy based on a self-government ideal.

The percentage of civil service employees recruited according to a neutral competence principle has steadily increased over the years in any society, and in the United State it reached more than 90% after both the Civil Service Reform Act signed by President Jimmy Carter in 1978 and the amendments enacted by the Supreme Court over the years to limit the externalities of partisan patronage (Ingraham & Ban 1984).[140] Nowadays, political patronage is less prevalent than in the past, since presidents now appoint less than 1% of all federal positions. Yet, this does not mean that patronage has lost all its relevance, since strategic appointments are still an important political means used by presidents to reward their supporters and to create a working relationship with members of congress.

In sum, the historical development of bureaucracy describes that this form of organization has become an essential feature for the management of complex modern societies. However, at the same time, bureaucracy transfers political power from the citizenry to technical officers, so the former may question the latter's power and they could request increased accountability and transparency in return for the transfer of power. That is, citizens want to have some form of control over the elites ruling government and other institutions and corporations. Above all, citizens want to know how governments are using the people's money, especially concerning taxpayer funds.

---

[140] Ingraham, P. W. and Ban C. (1984), *Legislating Bureaucratic Change: Civil Service Reform Act of 1978*, SUNY Press, New York.

One way of posing such control is to make bureaucrats accountable by requiring them to follow rules designed to treat people fairly, to refrain from politics on the job, and to fill out paperwork. However, these requests may also lead to unforeseen externalities, such as **the Red Tape issue**, which defines an excessive regulation or conformity to formal rules that is considered redundant and hinders action or other decision-making processes. This issue draws its name from the case in the 16th century when Henry VIII besieged Pope Clement VII with a significant amount of petitions for the annulment of his marriage to Catherine of Aragon. The pile of documents was rolled and stacked in original condition, each one sealed and bound with the obligatory red tape, as was the custom. Hence, the name red tape issue to describe an excessive amount of procedures to follow.[141]

The problem is thus that in order to respond to the people's request for accountability, civic service employees may be asked to fill out unnecessary paperwork, to obtain unnecessary licenses, to have multiple people or committees approve a decision and finally, to follow various minor rules that unavoidably slow down the whole bureaucratic process. In short, "red tape" indicates the governmental problem for which any official routine or procedure marked by excessive complexity results in delay or inaction. Therefore, governments must find a way to balance their need to get things done and to satisfy the people's need for transparency and accountability. To resolve this problem, the US government divided the federal bureaucracy in three branches: legislative, executive and judiciary.

12.3 Bureaucracy in the United States

The legislative branch drafts proposed laws, confirms or rejects presidential nominations for heads of federal agencies, federal judges and the

---

[141] Bozeman, B. (1993), "A theory of government "Red tape", *Journal of public administration research and theory*, 3.3, 273-304.

Supreme Court, it has the authority to declare war and finally, it also disposes of substantial investigative powers. American citizens have the right to vote for Senators and Representatives through free, confidential ballots. This branch includes a *Congress* composed of two parts: The Senate and the House of Representatives. In order to pass legislation and send it to the President for the signature, both these bodies must pass the same bill by majority vote (Little & Ogle 2006; 25-31).[142]

The Senate includes two elected senators per state for a total of 100 Senators, with the Vice-President serving as President of the Senate. These latter are in charge for a period of six years and their terms are staggered so that about 1/3 of the Senate is up for reelection every two years, even though there is no limit to the number of terms an individual can serve. Overall, the Senate is meant to confirm President's appointments that require consent, to provide advice on treaties' ratification, to impeach cases for federal officials and it has also to approve appointments to the Vice Presidency and any treaty that involves foreign trade.[143]

The House of Representatives has several powers, such as initiating revenue bills, impeach federal officials, and elect the President in the case of an Electoral College tie. This institution includes 435 elected Representatives, which are divided among the 50 states in proportion to their total population. There are additional 6 non-voting delegates who represent the District of Columbia, Puerto Rico and the territories. The presiding officer of the chamber is the speaker of the House and it is elected by other representatives. These elected officials serve a two-year term, and there is no limit to the number of terms an individual can serve.

The legislative branch encompasses also special agencies and offices that provide support services to Congress, the list of which includes agencies such as the Architect of the Capitol, the Congressional Budget

---

[142] Little, T. H., Ogle D. B. (2006), *The legislative branch of state government: people, process, and politics*, ABC-CLIO, California.

[143] The White House Government, "The Legislative Branch", retrieved at: https://www.whitehouse.gov/about-the-white-house/our-government/the-legislative-branch/

Office, the Congressional Research Service, the Copyright Office, the Government Accountability Office, the Government Publishing Office, the House Office of Inspector General, the House Office of the Clerk, the Joint Congressional Committee on Inaugural Ceremonies, the Library of Congress, the Medicaid and CHIP Payment and Access Commission, the Medicare Payment Advisory Commission, the Office of Compliance, the Open World Leadership Center, the Stennis Center for Public Service, the U.S. Botanic Garden, the U.S. Capitol Police and the U.S. Capitol Visitor Center.

Second, the **executive branch** carries out and enforces laws. Executive power is vested in the President of the United States, namely the individual in charge of leading the country. He or she is the head of state, leader of the federal government, and Commander in Chief of the United States armed forces. The president serves a four-year term and can be elected no more than two times. During his or her mandate, the president is responsible for implementing the laws written by Congress, while it is responsibility of the Cabinet and of independent federal agencies to take care of the day-to-day enforcement and administration of federal laws. These bureaucracies do so by providing regulations and restrictions on businesses and individuals, like limitations on allowable air pollution from factories, or the requirements that cars have airbags, or making sure that people do not have unfettered access to certain classes of drugs or overstay their visas.[144]

The president is supported by the Vice-president and when the former is unable to serve, the latter becomes president. The vice president can be elected and can serve an unlimited number of four-year terms as vice president, even under a different president. Vice-President is part of The Cabinet together with other advisors such as the heads of executive departments and other high ranking government officials. These advisors

[144] The White House Government, "The Executive Branch", retrieved at: https://www.whitehouse.gov/about-the-white-house/our-government/the-executive-branch/.

are nominated by the President and must be approved by a simple majority of the Senate.

Much of the work in the executive branch is thus done by executive departments, independent agencies and other boards, commissions, and committees. The most important executive department is 'The Executive Office of the Presidency' which was born in the New Deal expansion of federal power and that is aimed at coordinating the bureaucracy. The Executive Office of the Presidency (EOP) is home to agencies that the president appoints to help him manage the large range of issues that the White House has to deal with on a daily basis. This office – composed by different bodies such as the office of the President, the National Security Council, the Office of the United States Trade Representatives, etc. - is in charge of communicating the president's message and deals with the federal budget, security, and other high priorities.[145]

The office of the president cooperates with the **Executive Departments**, namely the 15 main agencies of the federal government that cover essential government functions or policy areas where clientele groups have been effective at lobbying for representation at the executive level, such as the U.S. department of Defense, Commerce, Justice, Labor and so on. The heads of these 15 agencies – also called "secretaries", except for the head of the Justice Department, who is called the "attorney general" are also members of the president's cabinet. These 15 main agencies are divided in Executive Sub-agencies and Bureaus, namely smaller sub-agencies aimed at supporting specialized work within their parent executive department agencies.

Finally, there are also independent agencies that are not represented in the cabinet and are not part of the Executive Office of the president, but which are structured similarly to other executive bodies with a presidential appointee at the top (some of whom can be fired by the president, and some of whom cannot). These bodies deal with government

---

[145] Branches of the U.S. Government, USA Government, retrieved at: https://www.usa.gov/branches-of-government.

operations and issues concerning the economy and regulatory oversight. In case there are areas that do not fall under these agencies (historic preservations, endangered species, Nuclear waste, etc.), Congress or the President can establish Boards, Commissions and Committees to manage these specific tasks. Even though they are not officially part of the executive branch, these bodies are also quasi-official agencies, namely organizations that are required by federal statute to release certain information about their programs and activities in the Federal Register, the daily journal of government activities.[146]

Overall then, the executive branch consists of several agencies as the president's cabinet, the departments under the responsibility of the cabinet members and all the agencies, boards, and commissions that put the laws of Congress into action. Moreover, these bodies also include everyone serving in the U.S. military and public corporations like the U.S. Post Office. Overall then, the Federal bureaucracy performs different central functions like diplomacy, defense, and internal affairs. Yet, these branches also perform 'minor' tasks such as responding to clientele groups of veterans, farmers, teachers, or other groups who feel that they have particular concerns.

Third, **the Judicial Branch** interprets the meaning of laws, applies laws to individual cases, and decides if laws violate the Constitution. It is composed of the Supreme Court and other federal courts. The former is the highest court in the United States, whose nine Justices – a Chief Justice and eight Associate Justices - are nominated by the president and must be approved by the Senate. To decide a case. there must be a minimum or quorum of six Justices, while if there is an even number of Justices and a case results in a tie, the lower court's decision stands. These

[146] Cohen, J. E. (1988), *The politics of the US cabinet: Representation in the executive branch, 1789-1984*. University of Pittsburgh Press, Pennsylvania.

Justices' service is not fixed term, since they serve until their death, retirement, or removal in exceptional circumstances.[147]

Together with the Supreme Court, the Constitution gives Congress the authority to establish other federal courts to handle cases that involve federal laws including tax and bankruptcy, lawsuits involving U.S. and state governments or the Constitution, and more. Other federal judicial agencies and programs support the courts and research judicial policy. The appointments for these federal judgeships follow the same basic process as the one for the appointment of Supreme Court Justices.

First, the President nominates a person to fill a vacant judgeship, then the Senate Judiciary Committee holds a hearing on the nominee and votes on whether to forward the nomination to the full Senate. If the nomination moves forward, the Senate can debate the nomination. Debate must end before the Senate can vote on whether to confirm the nominee. A Senator will request unanimous consent to end the debate, but any Senator can refuse. Without unanimous consent, the Senate must pass a cloture motion to end the debate. It takes a simple majority of votes - 51 if all 100 Senators vote - to pass cloture and end debate about a federal judicial nominee. Once the debate ends, the Senate votes on confirmation. The nominee for Supreme Court or any other federal judgeship needs a simple majority of votes - 51 if all 100 Senators vote - to be confirmed.

Therefore, these three sides of government are bureaucracies that perform essential tasks for the management of the United States, since they provide administration, rule-making which is filling in all the technical details in the laws Congress passes so that they can be enforced, and bureaucratic discretion when the bureaucracy exercises legislative power delegated to it by congressional law through judgment.

---

[147] The White House. "The Judiciary Branch", retrieved at: https://www.whitehouse.gov/about-the-white-house/our-government/the-judicial-branch/

CHAPTER 13

Political Parties and Interest Groups

Both political parties and interest groups are social bodies bound together by shared interests. Political parties are modern forms of factions in the sense that they seek goals particular to their interests. Interest groups have a shared vision to use the political system to attain their goals. Parties can develop higher degrees of cohesion in fragmented political systems. Interest groups use lobbying as a tool. Lobbying can be both direct and indirect; it is trying to persuade government officials to do something.

In countries with more than two parties, partisanship likely bows to practicalities and compromise. In the United States, it is challenging for third parties to get any relevant traction at the national level. There may be structural reasons that justify the maintenance of the two-party system in the United States. The Democrats and the Republicans dominate the national political spectrum today, which will likely remain so for the following years.

13.1 Parties and Interest Groups

Both political parties and interest groups are social bodies bound together by shared interests. They do their best to take advantage of the political system to accomplish their political goals. These are the factions James

Madison feared would be so destructive of democracy. The way they go about working the system to get political goals realized is very different.

Political parties are modern forms of factions in the sense that they seek goals particular to their interests. *Political parties* are groups bound by common interests which seek to use the political system to attain their goals from inside the system by controlling government. Different factors may affect and influence parties and interest groups' internal processes, such as choosing a favorite candidate and getting him elected. This form of *electioneering* is nominating and electing candidates to office. Once they are in office, they are *governing public officials* and run the political show.

Interest groups have a shared vision to use the political system to accomplish their goals. *Interest groups*, including corporations, are societies bound by common interests which endeavor to use the political system to achieve their policy goals by persuading inside people in power that will give them what they want. This form of action is known as lobbying. The act of persuading officials is a type of lobbying. It is typical for party representatives in government and interest group lobbyists outside the government to develop close working relationships where their interests overlap. These actions magnify their power.

13.2 The Role of Parties in a Democracy[148],[149]

What is involved with the duties of a political party? A political party must represent the interests of its members by gaining control of the

---

[148] For information on the role of political parties in socialist countries, see Corwin 11-24. Generally, in Cuba, as in China, only members of the Communist Party are allowed to vote or hold public office, and the party's most relevant members make all government decisions. Some exceptions to this rule may apply in China since the Asian country has a multiparty system, in which the Communist Party has authority over the rest.

[149] Under certain conditions, The Chinese political system allows for the participation of some non-CCP members (independents) and members of minor parties in the National People's Congress (NPC). The CCP is the only party that effectively holds power at the national level.

government. Parties have vital advantages and tools to strengthen and facilitate democracy in some crucial ways. Parties act as democracy-strengthening agents by providing a bridge and connection between voters and their elected officials.

Political parties also practice partisan politics. *Partisanship* is about identifying one's interests with a party's platform. Elected officials can be held accountable to the people who vote for them through re-election. *Accountability* is about ensuring our elected officials do what they say they are going to do. When a political party is helping to create accountability, they provide cohesion. Parties can develop higher degrees of cohesion in fragmented political systems. Parties also provide a voice to those in power, and they provide the opposition voice to those who are not in government.

13.3 Political Parties Create the Normality

Political parties create the normality that people countenance since they politically shape the social and cultural environment. The *responsible party model* is when political parties conform to paragons about how parties should ideally operate. One of these tools is the party platform. A *party platform* is a distinct set of policies based on a party's ideology, whose candidates align. People expect them to follow the party's platform and promises. If elected, citizens expect candidates to enact the values and policies of the party.

Voters make their choices based on the public policies political parties promote through their platforms; they are willing to vote against the party's candidates if they fail to keep their campaign promises successfully. Voters will likely reject party officials at the polls if party officials poorly carry out their partisan platforms' commitments. In the United States, the responsible party model is nothing but a yardstick against which actual parties can be measured.

United States parties can create unique party platforms different from each other in the political system. With several levels and branches, the national system offers many places where people and groups can engage the government. Candidates, in general, promise to support their party's platform if elected. People choose the political party they want to support through a process called partisan sorting. *Partisan sorting* identifies with the party because it most closely stands for their views and values and not for regional or other non-ideological reasons. Partisan sorting has historically been enforced by voters rather than by tight political party regulations. Increasingly, party members are not only partisan (that is, they identify with the political team); they are hyperpartisan.

Hyper-partisanship is when people are loyal to the party at all costs. Hyper-partisanship is an ideology that suggests that someone would choose their team over the other every time, even if it may require that they change their minds on policy priorities or values to do so. When voters are unwilling to vote against their party, even when it lets them down because the priority is to deny their opponents a win, they send a message to their party that it is acceptable not to keep promises.

To follow the dictates of the political party leaders to which they belong, House members and senators in the United States Congress may sometimes ignore the voters in their home states and the groups that represent them. For example, a member of the United States Congress from a state with a sizable elderly population may be inclined to vote in favor of legislation that will likely increase the benefits for retired people. However, their political party leaders, who disapprove of government spending on social programs, may ask for a vote against the legislation. The opposite can also occur, especially in the case of a legislator soon facing re-election. With two-year terms of office, it is more likely to see House members buck their party in favor of their constituents. (Corwin, 21)

13.4 Party Organization and Decision-Making

In liberal democratic countries, political parties no longer choose leaders in smoke-filled rooms behind the scenes. There is a formal and transparent process. Historically, *party machines* were organizations in which party leaders or "bosses" made the decisions and kept their voters' loyalty by providing them with services and support. Reforms included bringing party decisions, like whom to nominate, out of the proverbial "smoke-filled rooms." The way we are choosing political candidates today is in the smoke-free air of democratic transparency.

Political parties choose candidates through primaries and caucuses. *Primary elections*, often abbreviated to *primaries*, are processes by which voters can indicate their political preference for their party's candidate, or a general candidate, in an upcoming general election, local election, or by-election. *Primaries* are usually party-held preliminary elections.

A *caucus* is a meeting of political supporters or members (usually active) of a specific political party or movement. The definition of this term varies between countries and political cultures. *Caucuses* are the party gatherings where partisans debate candidate choices openly. While party officials still have a great deal of clout and resources, they are no longer "the boss."

Generally, political parties in the United States do not like nominating methods that allow non-party members to participate in selecting party nominees. In 2000, the United States Supreme Court heard a case brought by the California Democratic Party, the California Republican Party, and the California Libertarian Party. At the time, the parties argued that they had the right to determine who associated with the party and who participated in choosing the party nominee. The Supreme Court ultimately agreed to limit the states' choices for nomination methods to closed and open primaries.

13.5 A four-part party structure

The party structure rests in, more or less, four essential elements that make the party structure. The people in the electorate who identify with the party are people who vote party lines. These citizens are known as the *party followers* (1). On the other hand, *party activists* (2) are the party base, the most ideologically extreme of the party's voters. These activists are the ones that are the core group of people within the political party. *Party leaders* (3) are those who act as the official representatives of the political party.

The *party organization* is the official group, whose career party officials are part of it, that runs the party. This party organization is the functioning of the party within the state. Those who win an election are known as the *party-in-government members* (4) because they represent the people. *Party identification* is when people think of themselves as partisans (team members) and generally vote for the party. Identity politics are crucial to understanding national politics since political representation is, for some experts, rooted in the representatives' racial, ethnic, socioeconomic, gender, and sexual identity.

13.6 Why does the United States have a two-party political system?

In countries with more than two parties, partisanship likely bows to practicalities and compromise. If not, a party typically gets left out in the cold. In the United States, it is challenging for third parties to get any traction at the national level. There are structural reasons for the two-party system in the United States. The primary structural reason is that the United States does not have a proportional representation system, often found in parliamentary governments. The United States follows a *single member, first past the post district* model. These congressional districts in the United States have only one person elected—the person who gets the most votes.

The United States has made legal barriers to third parties to access federal funds. This situation implies that candidates are no longer dependent on the parties for their infrastructure. Third parties are vulnerable to the ability of social media to be manipulated and weaponized against them.

Third parties are cutting into fundraising against the major two parties. The parties are struggling to keep financial control in the age of the Internet. There is now much more opportunity for those not blessed by a major party's nomination to stage a campaign. Unlimited corporate and interest group funds are available to parties. A third-party candidate must get a certain number of signatures on a petition to get on the ballot in most states. Usually, when a third party begins to get traction, one of the parties will co-opt the winning issues.

13.7 The Parties Today

The Democrats and the Republicans dominate the United States political spectrum today. Democrats seek an activist government that believed it could and should solve economic and social problems at the national level. Republicans seek a hands-off, anti-regulatory business party. By the 1960s, Democrats had a solid hold on the United States Congress. *Richard Nixon's "southern strategy"* took advantage of race as a wedge issue to break conservative southern Democrats away from the Democrats and give the Republicans a majority.

Republicans seek a government that attends to its inherent responsibilities of maintaining a stable monetary and fiscal climate, encouraging a free and competitive economy, and enforcing law and order. Republicans seek a balance between the branches of government and every level. The Republican Party perceives that communism is the principal significant disturber of peace in the world today. Thus, they are reluctant to have relations with countries run by communist leaders and parties.[150]

The "new" Republican coalition began with the rise of evangelical Christian politics. Generally, traditional southerners were far more hierarchical, authoritarian, and evangelical-Christian than the average economic conservative Republican. The relationship between these two Republican groups ultimately led to considerable political friction because of broken promises and misunderstandings. For a time,

---

[150] For an in-depth analysis of the values of the two leading parties of the United States, see Donaldson, Robert. *Modern America: a Documentary History of the Nation Since 1945: A Documentary History of the Nation Since 1945*, 2014. London: Routledge. Internet resource.

economic conservatives paid lip service to social conservatives' concerns to keep the peace.

As one understands them today, national political parties did not exist in the United States during the republic's early years. At various points in the past 170 years in the United States history, national elites and voters have sought to create and foster alternatives to the existing party system. Political parties formed as alternatives to the Republican and Democratic parties are known as third parties or minor parties. Third parties, often born of frustration with the current political system, attract supporters from one or both of the existing and leading parties during an election but fail to attract enough votes to win. No third-party candidate has ever won the presidency, and historians still discuss why.

The Republican Party and the Democratic Party still have their economic and social left-right divisions. Trump's coalition's conservative social dimension is an interesting one, as critics argue that social conservatives seem to have set aside the traditional values that so motivated them in years past.

In the United States, two political movements formed fifteen years following John Kennedy's election: the American New Left and the American New Right. The New Left supports the call for social, economic, and political justice based on the equality of class, gender, and race than by the traditional leftist-Marxist dogma that socialism would replace the decadent capitalist system. On the other hand, the New Right focuses on downsizing the federal government, supporting state's rights, resisting communism, and reducing government regulations. Even if experts often describe both tendencies as radical movements, they are less orthodox than the traditional Left and the traditional Right.

13.8 Interest Groups' Basics

Madison's definition of factions can apply to both interest groups and political parties. Political parties and interest groups both work together and compete for social influence, although in different ways. Even though its writers did not mention the term interest group in the United States Constitution, the text's framers were aware that individuals would eventually band together in an attempt to use the governmental structure in their favor. One should especially consider that, while interest group activity often transcends political party lines, one can perceive many interests as more supportive of one party than the other. Thus, interest groups and political parties are related and may even closely work together as long as they support similar causes. For example, The American Conservative Union, Citizens United, the National Rifle Association, and National Right to Life will likely have relationships with Republican lawmakers than with Democratic ones.[151]

Interest groups do not need to be moderate—in fact, it is quite the opposite. The more stalwart and uncompromising interest groups stand on their positions, the better situated they are to draw a membership who shares their particular views. Individual citizens can join interest groups that promote and support the causes they favor.

Interest groups help provide representation to the people. The United States Constitution bases political representation almost entirely on geography. Interest groups give people a chance to get other interests they care about represented in government policy pursuing. Interest groups also help with political participation. *Political efficacy* is when people's sense of their ability to have a higher degree of control of their lives. Interest groups give people political participation opportunities that they would not typically have. Interest groups amplify the power of one. What one voice may not achieve, a chorus of multitudes may do much more quickly.

The role the interest groups provide in educating the public is essential. Interest groups usually provide information on their cause to policymakers by testifying in front of congressional committees, working with

---

[151] Corwin, Edward. "The Basic Doctrine of American Constitutional Law." *Michigan Law Review*, vol. 12, no. 4, 1914, pp. 247–276. *JSTOR*, www.jstor.org/stable/1276027. Accessed 8 Mar. 2021.

bureaucrats, or communicating directly with their members. Interest groups provide agenda building. By publicizing the values and interests they care about to the public and policymakers, interest groups can get onto their radar screens. This focus provides program alternatives and program monitoring.

13.9 Understanding Interest Groups

Interest groups can benefit society. Interest groups provide collective goods. *Collective goods* are benefits that, if the group is successful in obtaining them, can be enjoyed by everyone, whether they were members of the group and contributed to the purpose or not. There may be a problem with people who do not contribute to the interest group and only profit from it. *The free-rider problem i*s a quandary with getting people to join an interest group if they enjoy the benefit? Does a member get *material benefits* provided of actual monetary worth, like insurance discounts or professional paybacks? Are there *solidary benefits t*hat appeal to one's desire to associate with other people who care about the same things one does? Are there *expressive benefits* which are the opportunity to do work for something that matters deeply to one? Does the interest group provide *selective incentives* which benefit offered to induce people to join up?

We can understand interest groups' politics best if we think about the kinds of interests that bind their members together into different groups. *Economic interest groups* are those which seek to influence policy for the pocketbook issues of their members. On the other hand, *equal opportunity interest groups* pretend to influence the policymaking process by politically targeting citizens who feel unrepresented. These are different from public interest groups which aspire to change policy according to values that they consider are good for every citizen. *Government interest groups* are groups hired by governments to lobby other governments.

13.10 Interest Group Politics

What does one mean by "interest group politics"—are lobbyists politicians? Interest groups and their lobbyists are political actors in that they can bring considerable power to bear on elected officials. Power is relative amongst interest groups. Power can come from strength in numbers and resources.

Interest groups use lobbying as a tool. Lobbying can be direct and indirect. *Lobbying* is trying to persuade government officials to do something. *Lobbyists* are professionals who promote agendas and persuade public officials. *Direct lobbying* impacts public officials directly, while *indirect lobbying* focuses on the public to get the public to put pressure on public officials.

Professional lobbyists come from the ranks of professional politicians. There is a *revolving door* between lobbyists and politicians. The revolving door theory explains how people move from the public to the private sector and then sometimes back to the public sector. With direct lobbying of Congress, the Congress member's lobbyists focus on the committees and subcommittees that deal with the policies they mind. Interest groups research and investigate policy options and bring their findings to Congress members who cannot become experts on every topic they pass a law on.

Interest groups give money. *Political action committees (PACs)* can raise money but are limited in their contributions to candidates. One practical way for interest groups to increase their power is to form coalitions with other groups conveniently. Interest groups are as interested in influencing the people who implement the laws as they are interested in determining who makes them. The result is the public being shut out of the policymaking process, known as the Iron Triangle. Often, lobbyists, bureaucrats, and Congress members end up working together closely on laws affecting a particular sector that they finally come to identify with each other's interests. *Iron triangles* are the close policymaking relationships between legislators, regulators, and state-regulated groups.

Interest groups provide direct and indirect lobbying. Direct lobbying of the courts happens at the state level. State judges are frequently elected and willing to take campaign contributions. Lobbyists also operate in the Supreme Court and carry out their political mission by writing and submitting amicus curiae briefs on behalf of groups with interest in a particular case. Challenging a law in court is one way of lobbying the court to change the law. Indirect lobbying occurs when groups find it more beneficial to stay concealed behind an ostensible social movement. In these cases, they attempt to persuade the public to put pressure on our representatives.

People outside the political culture can lobby as well. When citizens become lobbyists, they are known as grassroots. Groups that orchestrate *grassroots lobbying* are usually those that arise from spontaneous popular movements and revolts. Fake grassroots movements are known as *Astroturf lobbying*. This lobbying type occurs through an orchestrated effort by an established interest group dressed up to look like a genuine popular movement. Astroturf lobbying is made more convenient by the Supreme Court rulings that say that spending money by individuals, groups, or corporations is a form of *protected free speech*.

CHAPTER 14

Media and Political Communication

People make decisions throughout their lives according to their perceptions and biases, eventually shaped by the information they receive from the media. News agencies influence our actions, judgments, and beliefs. Depending on how critical citizens are, media corporations will alter their perception of the world more or less. In countries like the United States, the government controls the media by the use of licensing. Reporting is not only about accurately reporting facts but also about increasing advertiser revenues and audience shares. Media outlets are looking to make a profit. Real reporting means digging out nuggets of truth and stitching them together into a coherent story that accurately informs the public of what is happening in their world. Ideally, in the entertainment and media industry, stories, pieces, and narratives are both fact-based and fact-checked. Respectable journalists do not write or spread fake news. Journalists can lose sight of what is necessary and still ethically acceptable for the sake of media sales and revenues.

14.1 Introduction to Media and Political Communication

How politicians and governments communicate with people occurs in all types of forms, such as the internet, books, television, and advertisements in mass media. The media can influence the governmental implementation of public policies and the development of public opinion. The media uses established communication channels for transmitting news, as well as influencing human behavior. The powerful complex of media technology not only carries information to us, but it also collects information about us.

The way media companies monitor and collect data about us creates a narrative and empowers companies. A significant component of power-building is control of the information or how one assembles data into narratives that influence public opinion. The rise of both cable and satellite television audiences translates into more options for media dissemination.

The phenomenal increase in channels through which information can flow for the informed citizen has made understanding the relationships among power, narratives, and political communication all the more central. The media are all-encompassing, enormously powerful and invasive, and yet, at the same time, more porous and open to our influence than ever before. The past decades have witnessed dramatic changes in the media environment, which have deepened during the social media revolution.

By intending to democratize political participation, social media has changed the way politicians, journalists, and public figures interact with the citizens. In real-time, social media users can respond to each other and influence public opinion. Citizens deliberate about policy-making in social media networks such as Facebook, Twitter, Instagram, Reddit, and more. Social media have these days the potential to both shape political campaigns and influence power relations in political parties as they allow candidates to campaign with a higher degree of independence than before.

14.2 Media Sourcing

The origin of media and the stories reported is a relevant aspect to verify. The roots of our thoughts and beliefs can be very blurry. Some media channels create their own stories through scientific reporting methods, while other sources merely report other news stories. A *media aggregator* is a channel that only picks and chooses from the reporting of others. Media aggregators do not always verify facts. They disseminate stories, even if the narrative is false.

Competent media reporting rests on reporting up to standards. *Reporting* in the media is the process by which professional journalists track down facts, check them, and ask hard questions, not settling for easy answers and pushing until they have found the truth. When looking for truth, the truth is not relative—it is verifiable with empirical (real-world) evidence. More and more news sites rely on using others' work, including the wire services like the Associated Press. Without the reporting of skilled, assiduous, and persistent journalists, our system would be in serious trouble.

Even though traditional forms of international diplomacy persist, one can see that modern hybrid wars also take place in the media. In this context, global public opinion is the prize. Governments, business organizations, religious-related entities, terrorist groups, and large-scale international NGOs pursue their political objectives by using the media. Throughout the world, public opinion is essential to the welfare of every government. Publicists do their best to create powerful narratives that are convincing enough for peoples all around the globe.

14.3 How we get and consume our news

A hallmark of authoritarian political systems is the state's effort to control the narrative by managing the press[152]. When the government controls the story, then truth can be relative to the media producer. He who controls the narrative-setting process also regulates what people think and feel

---

[152] On media biases and political repression, see Davenport, Christian. *Media Bias, Perspective, and State Repression: The Black Panther Party.* Cambridge University Press, 2010.

about something. Our media channels that seek out truth include word of mouth, print media, broadcast media, or electronic media sources.

Print media is in decline and it is struggling to figure out its role in the electronic world. The use of magazines and newspapers has evolved to appease today's audiences and advertisers. TV news, especially local news, still draws older generations, and its audience is dwindling. The internet is rapidly becoming the go-to place for people, predominantly the youth, to seek information.[153]

In today's busy world, we get in touch with the media from numerous sources and places. *Media convergence* is the process by which most of us get our news from many different sources. You may receive information from a multiplicity of news sources every day—paper, the internet, and television. People are becoming acclimatized to the media narrative in their life. A *mediated citizen*[154] is a citizen whose media dictate his lines of communication and thought. People live within a media bubble; however, it is possible to pop that bubble.

When people are comfortable in their information bubble, they are less likely to make changes. An *information bubble* is a person's media comfort zone, in which they listen to the news, curate social media, and meet new people, all of which reinforce the ideas they already have. Popping the bubble should be a fundamental goal of an educated person. We are vulnerable to manipulation tactics. Public opinion-influencing tactics leave us especially vulnerable to be controlled by those who guide the information we get. We live our lives according to the information we receive from the media. News agencies influence our actions, decisions, and beliefs.

---

[153] Newspaper revenues declined considerably between the years 2008 and 2018. Advertising revenue fell from $37.8 billion in 2008 to $14.3 billion in 2018, which evidences a 62% decline. For more information on this, see Grieco, Elizabeth. "Fast Facts about the Newspaper Industry's Financial Struggles as McClatchy Files for Bankruptcy." *Pew Research Center*, 14 Feb. 2020.

[154] On mass media depictions of citizens and the influence of those depictions, see Shumow, Moses. *Mediated Communities: Civic Voices, Empowerment and Media Literacy in the Digital Era.* Peter Lang, 2015.

Depending on how critical we are, the media will more or less be able to alter our perception of the world. They have the adequate tools to do so.

14.4 Media Ownership and Government Regulations

In the United States, the government does not own the media and news sources. Who owns media agencies if the government does not own them? And how does the government regulate the media? The government controls the media by the use of licensing. The government sells licenses to radio and TV stations and is now questioning the role social media plays in national security-related issues. Because of that, policymakers carefully examine which threats the media represent and boost. News agencies are big businesses all around the world.

Only in the United States, six corporations own most of the major media outlets. What difference does that fact make? How important is media ownership for us? How having little to no diversity in media ownership can affect us? Those who control the media are known as gatekeepers. *Gatekeepers* are the people in charge of what information gets to us, and most importantly, how it does. Today, most news comes from—or at least through—massive, corporate-owned sources. One can these days see a *commercial bias* in the media toward what will increase advertiser revenues and audience shares. When taking news stories and information from the media in a context that could be considered reliable, one should adequately contextualize and understand the media bias nature and the outlets' ideological and political views.

Having money, however, does not necessarily help when building effective political communication. Innovation and creativity play a crucial role in political communication, as in other forms of cultural integration, are not only a thing of the wealthy. Money certainly gives an advantage over the rest, but there are other factors that one should consider. Small and medium-sized news outlets can adjust to their budget and still create engaging and convincing narratives.

There is a continuous effort to get large audiences and keep them engaged. The media does that while also making way for increased advertising, which results in a reduced emphasis on political news, particularly for local television. Journalists lighten and dramatize the content of the information we get through the media. News is turned into *infotainment or soft news* to keep audiences tuned in and engaged.

Similarly, on the internet, infotainment is used to generate more news leads and story reads. *Clickbait* is the sensational headlines that tease you into clicking a link to find some intriguing-sounding information. By appealing to emotions and feelings, journalists aim to obtain more clicks from you. Today's media's corporate ownership means that the media outlets frequently face conflicts of interest in deciding what news to cover and how to cover it.

When doing their best to avoid getting "scooped" by another station or newspaper, reporters and editors alike sometimes jump the gun. Today, anyone can start a blog, a website, a podcast, or a YouTube Channel and start publishing his/her independent views. Social media networking has given voice to many new actors that influence public opinion.

If small media outlets and new-coming influencers look like they will be profitable, enterprising corporations likely have an incentive to scoop them up. Today, some outlets look like alternative media but have the funding of giants behind them. They are not independent at all. By appearing to be alternative or independent can attract new potential audiences that mistrust larger media outlets.

Media in the United States of America functions like a private enterprise system in which large businesses seek profit. The media in this country is almost entirely privately-owned, but they do not operate without some degree of public control. With fewer limitations on how many stations an owner can possess, the potential for media monopoly has become enormous over the years.[155]

---

[155] On media monopoly and the hilling effects of corporate ownership and mass advertising on the nation's news, see Bagdikian, Ben. *The Media Monopoly.* Beacon Press, 2000.. Since 1983, the number of corporations controlling most of America's daily newspapers, magazines, radio and television stations, book publishers, and movie companies has dwindled from fifty to ten to six.

The internet is known as a place in which the media can freely operate. However, that is only true as long as there is internet freedom in that country. Should the internet be regulated? Is it time to consider internet connectivity a basic human right? And are we prepared if it turns against us? Supporters of net neutrality believe that the internet should be an open-access forum for innovation. In the aftermath of Russian hacking and social media manipulation during the 2016 election, the internet has been up for scrutiny in Congress.

It is important to note that U.S. Congress members are mostly not among the generations that are internet savvy. It comes as no surprise that they often don't seem to know what they are searching for. Even though there has been significant-tech adoption since 2012 among older generations, Millennials still stand out for their technology use. On the other hand, Gen Z's are tech native.

14.5 What Do Journalists Do?

Both reporters and journalists gather information to later present it as news stories, feature articles, or documentaries. Journalists usually work on the staff of news organizations, but they work freelance as well. Freelance journalism means that they write stories for whoever pays them. General reporters cover all kinds of news stories, while other journalists specialize in specific areas such as politics, business, or fashion.

Journalists play a relevant, far-reaching, and essential role in our political system because they chase the news and deliver information to the rest of society. Valid-reporting means seeking answers. Reporting means digging out nuggets of truth and stitching them together into a coherent story that truly informs the public of what is happening in their world. Self-claiming that one is a journalist is not enough to be an authentic journalist. Citizens have to keep a keen eye on whether they contribute valuable, high-quality, factual, and not-strongly biased information to the public debate.

Journalism falls into four principal journalistic roles. The first role is to be a *gatekeeper* of truth. Editors and high-authority reporters who decide about what should be covered and what should not are the gatekeepers of truth for society. The second role is to be a disseminator. A *disseminator* is a reporter who mainly focuses on getting out facts rather than opinions. The third role of a journalist is to be a *researcher/analyst*. This type of journalist is a person who digs for information and interprets both its transcendence and significance by contextualizing it. The fourth type of reporter is a *public mobilizer*. This journalist usually has an agenda, and it is part of their job to make citizens aware of what is going on around them and encourage them to take action.

Journalists do not only communicate about what is going on in the world but also influence public opinion. In his seminal study of *Public Opinion*, Walter Lippmann observed that political action mostly derived from voting rights and mass media communications rather than from the collectively arrived at the will of rational, enlightened men. Citizens politically decide, more or less, through the exercise of the vote and the influence of public opinion. Lippmann recognized in 1922 that public opinion was a constructed and manufactured thing that could be shaped and manipulated by those with the resources and interests in doing so[156]. Publicists, press agents, and journalists are part of a social class situated between political organizations and media institutions. Their job is often to influence the public opinion-building process according to the needs of their clients.[157]

---

[156] On the role of news in the process of manufacturing public opinion, see Lipmann.

[157] For more information about how the press agents influence public opinion, see McNair, Brian. *An Introduction to Political Communication*. Routledge, Taylor & Francis Group, 2018. Political programs, policy agendas, electoral messages, pressure group campaigns, and acts of domestic and global terrorism have the potential for communicative effectiveness.

14.6 Issues, challenges, and controversies professional journalism faces

Professional journalists are often in a position that does not allow them to earn money from their work. It is too easy to make money off their work without paying them for it. News aggregators pose a threat to journalism because high-quality reporting costs both time and money. If a news source only retells another agency's story, the original story writer loses revenue for their work.

Another problem with professional journalism is that people have equated journalism with print journalism. Nowadays, people do not buy or subscribe to print outlets as they used to in the past. People object to paying for content online. There is a slow appreciation of electronic media. Major outlets are doing their best to maintain old business models based on subscription and print ad revenue while still successfully venturing into the digital world. As citizens distrust the media in general, it becomes more difficult for the public to trust the media. The public distrusts the media, which lacks credibility these days.

Respectable journalists do not write fake news. Fake news is out there, but credible journalists do their best to confront it. What is distinctive about good journalism is the reporters' commitment to accuracy, objectivity, and detail in telling their stories. Journalists have to properly research and verify their facts because they act as communicators who work in service of the truth, even if it is troublesome.

Low-quality journalism may allow disinformation and misinformation to originate in or leak into the news industry, which is likely to mislead public opinion. Strong ethical journalism and professional standards are required as antidotes to both disinformation and misinformation. As long as we do not control the avalanche of disinformation, the public may come to disbelieve all content, including journalism. Citizens are likely to take as credible whatever content their close friends and preferred influencers share in social networks. Disinformation campaigns do not necessarily aspire to convince the public to believe that its content is veracious but rather impact the agenda-setting. Fake news can shape what people think is relevant and what is not.

One should consider that when people use the phrase "fake news," for the most part, what they are trying to do is to control the narrative. Fake news accusations are used as a way of delegitimizing a journalist's work. Because of its popularity, the term has recently been weaponized to leverage attacks against the media. Citizens may use the term "fake news" to satisfy their need for structure in the world. Cognitively speaking, people need to satisfy their need to see the world around them as an orderly, coherent, and structured place rather than solely to express their political, cultural, or personal ideology. One can already see the negative impacts of this situation on public beliefs about health, science, and intercultural affairs.

News organizations in the United States recognize fake news as a sociopolitical problem while acknowledging the challenge in defining it because of its many uses and connotations depending on the context. In general, specialists consider fake news as a social media phenomenon thriving on political polarization driven by mostly ideological and partisan, but sometimes also cultural and financial motivations. It has become common throughout the world to blame for the rise of fake news to the current political environment, to technological platforms Google, Twitter and Facebook, and some particular audiences as well.

14.7 Media Shapes The Political Narrative

The media has historically played an integral role in influencing social trends. The information era, a new history term used to capture the way the world has recently developed to rely on information for most of the actions that people take, remains significantly different from all the other periods in the history of humankind.

More than ever, information and narratives now have significant powers to change and influence the way people think and act. Most importantly, the reasoning they help portray on various relevant topics in society. The media is essential to push for specific narratives and messages in the modern world.

The contemporary media industry has emerged as the most advanced system of communication that humanity has ever experienced. Unlike in the past, when information and narratives could take long periods to reach citizens, the situation is radically different in our times since information travels the world in seconds. Researchers have studied the role of the contemporary media in political driving narratives quite extensively. The media drives our social, economic, and political trends. Communication outlets influence the reasoning that people hold as truths.

The primary purpose of the mass media outlets is to tell convincing yet engaging stories. Ideally, in the media industry, stories and narratives are not only fact-based but also fact-checked. And who exactly are the storytellers? At the pinnacle of political reporting are the Washington press corporations. Some of them have been politicians or at least members of the political world. As politicians move from the political to the private sector, the list of government officials regularly changes. This *revolving door-like process* consists of moving from the political sector to the public or the private ones. Some journalists are ethically stellar, but others' loyalty may lie more toward their political allies than their audiences.

14.8 Media and politicians will try to create a narrative line and spin the facts that fit the narrative

When a politician *spins* a story, they are likely to purposely select pieces of information that fit their political narrative and intentionally interpret data to make things look different by distorting facts and ignoring relevant factors. In political journalism, spins are attempts to control communication to deliver one's preferred message and persuade audiences. The term is commonly used to refer to the sophisticated art of promoting one's agenda by selling and spreading specific messages in favor of one's interests and views. Political spins often imply a certain degree of deception. A person who offers to give their opinion or commentary to mass media outlets on a particular subject area (most typically *political analysis*) is a pundit. A *pundit* is a person who can sometimes fall into the "analyst" category of journalists and sometimes into the bloviator category. The journalist can spin a story through different methods.

Journalists can spin a tale by creating an agenda for their news source and creating an important story that people focus on. *Agenda setting* is what a journalist, editor, or producer decides is important becomes news and ends up on the political agenda.[158] This agenda-setting can frame issues so that one or two topics become relevant in the national discussion for the day. *Framing* the political debate and public opinion is about telling people what matters the most and what to pay attention to when reading the news. There should be a reliance on skilled and professional communicators who stick to engaging, easy, and already existing narratives to shape and influence political debates.

Journalists can lose sight of what is necessary for the sake of media sales and revenues. A *feeding frenzy* is a process by which a scandal turns average journalists into sharks-like beings waiting for the next tidbit of news to drop. This situation can cause trouble when people focus on scandal and clickbait instead of seeking the truth. During election cycles, it is a common problem to only focus on the person winning a race. This *horse race-type of journalism* in election reporting focuses on who is ahead, who is losing support, and who is a surprisingly long shot, but not on the substance of what the election is really about. Much of the time, the end result is the *soundbite* generated, which is a short and snappy memorable line that commentators may repeat over and over. Often, they do so by taking facts out of context.

---

[158] See Zaller, John. *The Nature and Origins of Mass Opinion.* Cambridge University Press, 2011 for more information on the tactics to influence public opinion throughout history.

CHAPTER 15

Domestic Policy

15.1 Introduction to Policy

A **policy** is a prescribed course of action for those who work for the government. It creates a set of operational principles through which to accomplish desired goals.

Setting **domestic policy** creates standard operational procedures by which a government operates. Policies are put in place to guide the bureaucratic agencies that work under the Executive Branch.

When governments create laws and policies, either domestic or foreign, it is called policymaking. **Policymaking** is the process by which the Congress creates public policies. A **public policy** is a government plan of action to solve a problem that people share collectively or that they cannot solve on their own. These public policies are meant to create solutions to problems for the greater good of society. We can understand public policy as a purposeful course of action intended by officials to solve problems of society.

15.2 Making Public Policy

The power to make public policy in the United States begins with Congress. Policies are usually created by legislators in the form of new proposals or bills, which are passed by both the House and Senate and signed into law by the president. The role of influencing and creating public policy also resides in limited form within the Executive Branch.

A president may also create policy through multiple pathways: by placing an issue on the public agenda, including in their budget proposal, vetoing a law passed by Congress, or issuing an **executive order** that establishes a new policy or augments an existing one. Executive orders are directed only to government bureaucracies at the federal, state, or local levels. These agencies can wield enormous control over policy through how they enforce such orders.

The court system also can make public policy. When a court rules on what the government can, should or should not do, it is clearly taking an active policy making role. The courts, especially the **Supreme Court**, can create public policy by hearing cases that change policy adoption, allow for policy to be formulated, or create standards by which we interpret public law.

15.3 Types of domestic public policy

Scholars have come up with a typology of domestic problems that require different kinds of policies to solve them. These categories help determine the types of social and economic policies that the nation adopts.

The method by which a policy is implemented may vary according to the type of economic and political policy. Some policies are considered redistributive in nature. These **redistributive policies** use resources from affluent segments of society to provide benefits for those less likely to participate in the political sector. Redistributive policies are less likely to occur in more capitalistic market systems.

Domestic policies that are equally taxing on all of the population are called distributive in nature. A **distributive policy** is one whose costs are borne by the entire population. An example would be a flat-based tax system that is the same across all income brackets.

Some domestic policies, however, do not deal with the allocation of goods and resources in society. A domestic policy that does not distribute resources but exerts control within society through behaviors it requires is called a regulatory policy. **Regulatory policies** control behavior rather than distributing resources.

15.4 Social Policy

Many domestic policies are designed as social policies. **Social policies** are primarily distributive and redistributive policies that improve Americans' quality of life. If a social policy is distributive or redistributive for social welfare needs, it is a **social welfare policy,** a government program designed to provide for those who cannot, or sometimes will not, provide for themselves. Those programs that care for those who cannot care for themselves are the most redistributive in nature. Often there are rules and requirements, usually based on income potential.

Social policies that filter who is eligible or not for the redistribution of wealth often utilize means-tested programs. **Means-tested programs** require that beneficiaries prove they lack the necessary income or resources to provide for themselves, according to the government's definitions of eligibility. This is usually based on income-earning potential. In the United States, these types of programs often carry a social stigma and are contentious during elections.

Certain types of means-tested social programs are designed to help families in need. One example is the **Temporary Assistance to Needy Families (TANF)** program that replaced AFDC. This program provides block grants to state governments, giving states greater control over how they spend their money. The TANF program caps the amount that the federal government will pay for welfare and requires work in exchange for time-limited benefits. Other requirements may include recipients finding jobs within two years, then removing them from welfare rolls after a total of five years or less, depending on the state.

Another domestic policy program for helping people who make less than a federally legislated income level is the **Supplemental Nutrition Assistance Program (SNAP).** SNAP is the largest United States food assistance program for low-income families, providing vouchers to purchase food. This program helps those without enough resources for food and sustenance.

In modern times, many Americans are unaware that the policy we have referred to for years as "welfare" is mostly gone.

One of the best-known social policies is Social Security Insurance. **Social insurance policies** are longer-term distributive programs that provide benefits to a specific segment of the population. **Social Security** is a program born in the Great Depression to provide retirement funding for the elderly. It works through an economic input, or buy-in, when workers pay into the federally backed program. People contribute to Social Security during their working lives in order to receive benefits after they retire. Current workers pay the Social Security of retirees, with any leftover money going into the Social Security trust fund. Most people, at least those who are older, see Social Security as something they have earned and to which they are entitled, not as a government handout.

Still, there are problems with Social Security. With longer life spans, most people end up getting much more back from Social Security and Medicare than they may have contributed. Many workers who have paid into the system see Social Security as an entitlement. **Entitlement programs** require benefits to be paid to people who are entitled to receive them. They are not needs-based nor do they follow a means-tested approval system. Even though there is talk of the Social Security system going insolvent, it could be made sustainable. Some potential remedies, however, are politically unpalatable and vigorously opposed by interest groups, including the American Association of Retired People (AARP).

Domestic policies to ensure the health care of people are increasing. The **Patient Protection and Affordable Care Act** established and made access to health insurance more available and affordable for most Americans. The United States stands out among industrialized nations as the only one that doesn't have a universal health-care system guaranteeing minimum basic care to all. Historically, healthcare in America pre-2010 utilized Medicare (covering old people) and Medicaid (covering the poorest people) for health care coverage of those without insurance. The consequences were that many uninsured people fell through the cracks.

Medicare was a social insurance program designed to help the elderly pay their medical costs. This program has been modified since the inception, however, it is still focused on elderly care. Medicare has become an extraordinarily expensive program. **Medicaid** is a means-tested welfare program designed to assist the poor -- especially children -- with their medical costs. This program undergoes adjustments when domestic policies allow for increased coverage and care for different segments of society.

15.4 Economic Policy

Government creates economic policies to keep the economy stable, growing, and functioning smoothly. **Economic policies** include all the different strategies that government officials, elected and appointed, employ to solve economic problems, to protect economic rights, and to provide procedural guarantees to keep the financial markets running smoothly. The government can control and regulate the marketplace or allow it to go mostly unregulated, with each approach depending on the political policy and party in power.

The consequences of a largely unregulated market vary. More regulation of the commerce of food and energy can increase the cost of goods and services for consumers. Traditionally, policymakers have felt that the government should pursue a hands-off economic policy. This allows for consumers to decide how much they are willing to pay for goods and services. Since the Great Depression, the goal of economic policymakers has been to even out the dramatic cycles of inflation and recession without undermining the vitality and productivity of a market-driven economy. America has gone through various series of recessions, depressions, and economic growth, often influenced by the domestic policies set by the government.

Economic policies are complicated, so for the sake of brevity we will provide a short and simple description. The government uses fiscal policy to grow or shrink the economy through taxation. **Fiscal policy** is the government's power to tax and spend with the aim of stabilizing the economy. This is done to create both surpluses and deficits in national spending. A **surplus** is money saved after spending on the government's domestic policy. A **deficit** is money owed after spending beyond what is actually available.

There are many tools available to create a healthy fiscal policy. One power of the government is known as monetary policy. **Monetary policy** is the power to control the money supply by manipulating interest rates. When interest rates are low, people can borrow money at a lower cost, spurring more business activity. The monetary policy of the United States is run by the **Federal Reserve System (the Fed)**. The Federal Reserve System is a group of 12 banks run by a board of governors whose chair is appointed by the president. It sets interest rates for the nation and is autonomous of the Executive Branch or Congress.

The government has the power to take from every citizen and business a share of their revenue for the purpose of ensuring the national interest. Taxation is the power to charge people a percentage of their income for the domestic and foreign policy needs of the government. **Tax policy** is the way in which the government requires that individuals and businesses contribute to collective costs. Taxation levels may be different for people depending on their income levels. A **progressive income tax** is a tax on people with more money at a higher rate than the rate applied to people with less money. This is different from a **regressive tax.**,. A regressive tax may take a higher percentage of a poorer person's gross resources, like sales taxes or value-added taxes (VATs) or some proposals for a flat income tax. There are other types of taxes as well, including **capital gains taxes**, a controversial tax that may be levied on the return from capital investments.

15.5 Environmental Policy

President Richard Nixon in 1970 signed a National Environmental Policy Act that a year later became the **Environmental Protection Agency**, or EPA. During the 1970s, laws were passed regarding clean air and clean water, as well as protections for endangered species. With these, sources of air and water pollutants came under federal regulation. Environmental policy attempts to balance the protection and conservation of natural resources with economic growth and jobs. Industries are required to follow federal and state rules designed to protect the natural environment. The rigor with which these regulations are enforced often depends on the political party in power at any particular time. For example, President Ronald Reagan in 1982 cut EPA funding by 30 percent.

The **Department of the Interior** was established in 1849 to manage natural resources, and oversees energy development on federal lands as well as offshore leases. A division, the **Bureau of Land Management**, was formed in 1946 to manage the federal lands that total almost 250 million acres.

15.6 Energy Policy

U.S **energy policy** is sometimes connected to environmental policy, especially when energy production and consumption involves the exploitation of natural resources and creates pollutants. Legislation, regulations, international treaties, subsidies and taxation are all modes of policy implementation. Coal, oil, natural gas, hydroelectric and nuclear power, and more recently renewables including wind and solar power have powered America through the years and been subjects of energy policies. Fossil fuels still account for most United States energy consumption. Federal tax policies and subsidies can be used as incentives for the development of specific energy sources.

There is concern in the United States and worldwide over greenhouse gas emissions that are related to climate change. China and the United

States are the biggest carbon polluters, and many nations and industries are taking steps to reduce such emissions and move toward energy efficiencies and renewable sources, though there has been no firm global agreement on such policies as yet.

15.7 Health Policy

America's massive and complex health-care industry accounts for about 17 percent of all spending, mostly on medical services to diagnose and treat illnesses and injuries, both physical and mental. **Health policy** has therefore become a contentious issue between political parties and is often adjusted, depending on who is in power. The United States system is a third-party payer arrangement in which health insurance companies reimburse medical providers a portion of the cost of services to patients. Almost half of Americans participate in private health insurance plans through their employers. Medicare (15 percent), for people over 65, and Medicaid (16 percent), for low-income people, are public programs touched on earlier under social policies. While the Affordable Care Act, also known as Obamacare, has helped expand coverage since its passage in 2010, there are still about 30 million (13 percent) of Americans who are uninsured, mostly because of the high costs of healthcare. Soaring costs have also driven employers to reduce the reimbursements paid to medical providers and to increase the burden of insurance premium payments on their employees.

15.8 Transportation Policy

The Department of Transportation (DOT) plans and coordinates federal transportation projects to enhance national economic competitiveness, facilitating the movement of people and goods and also setting safety regulations for all major modes of transport, including air, water, and land – both roads and railways. **National Transport Policy** also attempts to reduce negative impacts on the environment.

The Federal Aviation Administration, Highway Administration, Railroad Administration, Transit Administration and other agencies are related to the DOT.

Many federal infrastructure programs and policies have failed to modernize in recent decades, according to DOT research, leading to five major challenges, which involve crumbling infrastructure, congestion, climate change, injuries and fatalities as well as unequal economic opportunity.

Transportation is the biggest source of United States greenhouse gas emissions, with more than 100 million people living amid pollution that exceeds health-based air quality standards. Traffic congestion costs the economy more than $165 billion in wasted productivity and fuel each year. Additionally, many infrastructure assets including highways, public transit and rail systems have come to the end of their useful lives and require repair or replacement. New modes of transport will also be necessary to handle the demands of both the economy and the environment in the future.

CHAPTER 16

Foreign Policy

16.1 Foreign policy

Foreign policy determines how the United States reacts and responds to governments and non-governmental groups beyond its borders. **Foreign policy** is the official policy designed to solve problems that occur between the United States and actors from abroad. It is important to have successful policies for national self-preservation. Without a strong and effective foreign policy, America's security as a rich and peaceful country could come under threat. Although the United States has little control over the other actors involved. its foreign policy is generally carried out for the good of American citizens or in the interest of national security.

16.2 Two fundamental perspectives on our relationship with the world

Relationships with other nations can be seen through two distinct perspectives: isolationism and interventionism. **Isolationism** is a foreign policy view holding that Americans should put themselves and their problems first and not interfere in global concerns. The United States pursued an isolationist policy after World War I, but this experiment was seen largely as a failure. The second fundamental perspective is **interventionism**, which holds that to keep the republic safe, the United States must be actively engaged in shaping the global environment and willing to intervene in order to create desired outcomes.

16.3 Foreign policy and external actors

Many organizations are external actors within the current foreign policy environment. Intergovernmental organizations are bodies that have countries as members, including the United Nations, NATO, OPEC, and the EU. These international bodies work together to create agreements among nations regarding international policies. American foreign policy relies on the concept of **American Exceptionalism**, which teaches that the United States is unique, marked by a distinct set of ideas including equality, self-rule, and limited government. The aim of foreign policy is to create a commonly held theory of democratic peace teaching that democratic nations are less likely to engage in wars with one another

The president is the chief negotiator for the United States, and any treaty negotiated must then be ratified by the Senate. The president has ample resources available to fulfill the obligations of the office. The **National Security Council (NSC)** is the president's inner circle that advises on matters of foreign policy and is coordinated by the national security adviser. Foreign policy is negotiated through the **Department of State, which** is charged with managing foreign affairs. The secretary of state is part of the president's cabinet and fulfills a variety of foreign policy roles, including maintaining diplomatic and consular posts around the world, sending delegates and missions (groups of government officials) to a variety of international organization meetings, and negotiating treaties and executive agreements with other countries. The **Department of Defense (DOD)** manages the United States military and its equipment in order to protect the nation. It is headed by the secretary of defense, and under that office are the **Joint Chiefs of Staff**, service chiefs of the Army, Navy, Marine Corps, Air Force, Space Force, and the National Guard Bureau. While the chief of the Coast Guard is not an official member of the Joint Chiefs, a Coast Guard admiral routinely meets with the group.

The Defense Department is the government's biggest agency and accounts for a large portion of the national budget, along with health spending and Social Security. It employs almost 3 million service members and civilians in more than 160 countries and is headquartered in the iconic Pentagon building in Arlington, Virginia, just outside Washington DC.

16.4 Trade policy

United States **trade policy** objectives in recent decades have included reducing protections both at home and abroad, opening foreign markets for American exports, and increasing global economic integration. While there has much success in integrating the world's economies, the United States has seen its share of the gross world product (GWP) plummet since the post-war period, and its position as the world's biggest economy challenged first by Japan in the 1990s and now by China, which is expected to overtake it in the future. America's international trade deficit now routinely exceeds $600 billion annually, as the United States buys far more foreign goods and services than it sells.

The **Department of Commerce** is charged by the president with helping the economy expand through working to ensure fair trade and providing the data necessary to support commerce. It also helps negotiate bilateral trade agreements, enforces laws and issues sanctions that attempt to ensure a level playing field for United States businesses.

Even more directly concerned with trade policy is the office of the **United States Trade Representative** (USTR), which is responsible for developing and recommending trade policy to the president. It also conducts trade negotiations for the executive branch and participates in the World Trade Organization (WTO).

Tariffs are customs duties levied on imported and exported goods and services. They are typically used to protect domestic industries or as leverage in trade negotiations and disputes. While Congress originally had the power to levy tariffs granted by the Constitution, the president has the power to negotiate international agreements, so Congress has partially delegated to the executive the latitude to negotiate trade agreements and set **tariff policy**. The United States has been a member of the WTO since 1995, and as such makes tariff policies within the regulatory context of the global trading system.

Tariffs are actually a type of tax paid on goods sourced from other countries and usually paid to United States customs authorities by importing companies. While tariffs may offer some protection to domestic industries by raising prices of competing imported goods, they are ultimately paid by United States consumers to whom cost increases are passed by importers.

About the Author

R. L. Cohen is a university lecturer residing in Redlands, California. His research focus is on political science, ethics, and religious studies. When he is not lecturing, he often can be found at the beach, at a unique coffee bar, or traveling back to his home in New Zealand.

Printed in the USA
CPSIA information can be obtained
at www.ICGtesting.com
LVHW022207200224
772410LV00003B/10

9 781988 557632